The Narrow Way

Examining Both Heaven and Hell and
the Message of Eternal Salvation in Jesus Christ

William C. Nichols

International Outreach, Inc.
P.O. Box 1286, Ames, Iowa 50014 USA

*With special thanks to **Melvin J. Swenson**,*
the man who first got me involved in personal evangelism.
He has been a constant encouragement and inspiration to me
and has faithfully edited all of my manuscripts.

Unless otherwise noted, Scripture taken from the New American Standard Bible, © 1960, 1962, 1963, 1968, 1971, 1972, 1973, 1975, 1977, by the Lockman Foundation. Used by permission.

First Printing of *The Narrow Way* 1993

International Outreach, Inc.
PO Box 1286, Ames, Iowa 50014 USA

The Narrow Way
Contents

Chapter

TO THE READER:

Constantly in His discourses with men, the Lord Jesus Christ spoke of eternal realities. Christ frequently spoke of hell, heaven, death, the judgment, and sin and the necessity of repentance from all sin, for these are among the few subjects which will cause men whose hearts and minds are set on the world to consider eternity. In the parables of the sower and the soils, the wheat and the tares, and the wise and foolish virgins the Lord taught men the danger of presuming they were saved when they might not be. In His discourse of the broad and the narrow roads Christ warned men that the way to heaven was hard and that few find it.

These are timeless subjects and men are probably in greater need of hearing about them today than perhaps ever before because heaven, hell, the difficulty of obtaining eternal life, and the danger of false conversion are rarely spoken of in our day. Since it is my conviction that men have a need to hear of them, they are the subjects of this book.

It is my desire in the pages of this book to set forth a biblical view of heaven, hell, God, and man and to proclaim the gospel of Jesus Christ in plain terms. I will not seek to withhold the hard teachings of Christ and the Scriptures, for this would not help any, and indeed, would hurt many and might contribute to their ultimate damnation. Please read this work in its entirety with an open heart and a prayerful spirit of self-examination (II Corinthians 13:5). It is my firm conviction and constant grief that *many* today who profess to be Christians will one day hear those terrifying words of Christ: "Depart from Me, ye cursed, into everlasting fire, prepared for the devil and his angels" (Matthew 25:41). Are you willing to risk that you might be one of them?

Dear Reader, you will be in this life only for a brief period. In a very short time all who can now read this book will be in heaven or hell, there to reside eternally. Will you give no thought to life after death now? Will you refuse to prepare now for your eternal abiding place while you have opportunity? For the sake of your soul, read the pages of this book with the realization that if you are deceived about your condition before God and die in an unrepentant and unconverted state you shall dwell in the fires of hell forever. Your eternal well-being may depend upon it.

William C. Nichols
July 22, 1993

1

The Glory of Heaven

*"Then the King will say to those on His right, 'Come,
you who are blessed by My Father, enter the kingdom
prepared for you from the foundation of the world'"
(Matthew 25:34).*

"When a mortal man speaks anything of that eternal blessedness of
the Saints in glory, he is like a blind man discoursing about the light
which he has never seen, and so cannot distinctly speak anything
concerning it."[1] Likewise, for one to write of those things which are
only vaguely described in Scripture is similar for a man to write a
travel guide for a land he has never visited or seen. It is to attempt to
describe the indescribable with words which cannot come close to
expressing the glory of heaven. Paul wrote these words: "Things
which eye has not seen and ear has not heard, and which have not
entered the heart of man, all that God has prepared for those who love
Him" (I Corinthians 2:9). Some question whether these words directly
refer to heaven: they may not, but from all that we do know, they are
certainly true of heaven and of the indescribable nature of that glorious
place. Things which eye has not seen: can you imagine it? Men's eyes
have seen abundant treasures upon the earth. Men have seen golden
thrones, palaces, exquisite diamonds, rubies, and pearls. Men can
conceive of handfuls of diamonds, fields of jewels, and buildings of
gold, glittering in the noonday sun, but men cannot imagine the glory
of heaven. It is beyond our imagination. Such is the task before us: to
speak of the glory of heaven using words that cannot describe it; to try
to picture for you that which cannot even be conceived by your heart.

Why be so concerned about heaven? What purposes will be served
by doing so? There are several reasons which make it profitable to both
hear and think about heaven: 1) The doctrine of heaven serves to
comfort true believers on earth who are weary and struggling or under
persecution. 2) Hearing of heaven should stir up believers to witness
to friends and neighbors on earth who are not followers of Jesus Christ.
Meditating on the glory of heaven and the frightening alternative
should be one of the greatest incentives to evangelism there can be.
And 3) The concept of rewards for obedience and of punishment for
disobe-dience is a major theme throughout all of Scripture. Why

would God do this if it were not to urge otherwise senseless men to consider eternity before it is too late? Hearing about heaven then is an incentive to the ungodly to turn to God now while there is still time. We will speak in more detail of these later. Let us now try to understand what the Bible tells us about what heaven is like.

A DESCRIPTION OF HEAVEN

Heaven is a place of unspeakable glory where the elect of God live with one another in the immediate presence of God and of the Lamb and where they behold Him in all His glory face to face. It is a place where the curse of sin and all of its effects have been removed forever from all who dwell there; they, being made joint heirs with Christ, inherit all things and live with unmixed joy in a state of perfect happiness incapable of being described or exaggerated forever and ever.

Heaven is called by Jesus Christ "a kingdom." "Come you who are blessed of My Father, inherit the kingdom prepared for you from the foundation of the world" (Matthew 25:34). It is called "the kingdom of God" (Acts 14:22). This tells us that the exceeding glory of this kingdom far outweighs the glory of all earthly kingdoms combined. This is a heavenly kingdom where Christ is King. Not only that, but those who live there with the Blessed One are declared by Christ to be "priests to His God and Father" (Revelation 1:6) and proclaimed by Peter as "a chosen race, a royal priesthood, a holy nation, a people for God's own possession" (I Peter 2:9). What kingdom is like unto this kingdom? What earthly kingdom can be compared to it? There are none.

Heaven is called "the third heaven" (II Corinthians 12:2) and "the heaven of heavens" (Deuteronomy 10:14) to show its great eminency. By this it is distinguished from the sky above, the atmospheric heaven, which is also called heaven, and the starry heaven containing all the celestial orbs: the sun, the stars, the planets, and moons of the universe. Think how vast and great are the starry heavens above. The heaven of heavens is far greater still. Here we see only the objects of creation. There God's children will see, worship, and dwell with the God who *created* the universe and everything in it.

In the parable of the unrighteous steward, Christ refers to heaven as "the eternal dwellings" or as one version translates it "the everlasting habitations" (Luke 16:9). This tells us that heaven is a place, not a dream or an illusion. It is a place where glorified saints and angelic beings live together with God. We are told that God "has prepared a city for them" and we are given a preview of the glory of this city in Revelation 21: "Her brilliance was like a very costly stone, or a stone of crystal-clear jasper...the city was pure gold, like clear glass. The foundation stones of the city wall were adorned with every kind of precious stone...And the twelve gates were twelve pearls; each one of the gates was a single pearl. And the street of the city was pure gold, like transparent glass...the city has no need of the sun or of the moon to shine upon it, for the glory of God has illumined it, and its lamp is the Lamb." It is also a place that remains forever. It is called "eternal" or "everlasting" and of its inhabitants it is said, "neither can they die anymore, for they are like the angels, and are sons of God" (Luke 20:36). Those who go to heaven live in that glorious city for all eternity.

When Christ was dying on the cross the penitent thief next to Him made a request of the Lord: "Jesus, remember me when You come in Your kingdom!" Christ responded to him: "Truly I say to you, today you shall be with Me in Paradise" (Luke 23:42 & 43). Heaven is called Paradise. Men often refer to an exotic, tropical island as "paradise," yet this paradise will make all earthly paradises look meager and barren.

In Luke 16 heaven is also called Abraham's bosom. Christopher Love helps us understand this expression better: "Dives saw Lazarus in Abraham's bosom. And it is so called, because as the bosom is the receipt of love, and the friend of your bosom is your dearest friend, so in glory they are said to be in Abraham's bosom to show that God will love and shelter His elect, as a friend will do to this dearest friend, the friend of his bosom."[2] This is Paradise indeed!

Lastly, heaven is called "the joy of your master." The servant who acted wisely with his master's talents is welcomed into the kingdom of God with these words: "Well done, good and faithful slave; you were faithful with a few things, I will put you in charge of many things; enter into the joy of your master" (Matthew 25:23). Psalm 16:11 tells us: "In Thy presence is fulness of joy; in Thy right hand there are pleasures forever."

These expressions have given us a view of heaven which is like looking through a colored glass at a far distant kingdom which we cannot see clearly. Now we will look at the blessedness of heaven from two different perspectives. The first one will show us what those in heaven will be free from. The second will give us a better understanding of what the eternal blessedness of the soul consists.

The occupants of heaven shall be freed from sin itself, from the causes of sin, and from the consequences of sin. First, those who enter glory to live forever with God in heaven shall be free from sin itself.

Sin is the cause of all the misery in the world. Sin is the reason we experience pain, sorrow, sickness, and even death. Paul mourns over sin and expresses in strongest language his desire to be rid of it: "Wretched man that I am! Who will set me free from the body of this death?" (Romans 7:24). The true child of God longs to be where he will sin no more: a place where he will never commit another sin; a place where he will never even have another sinful thought. Sin is the greatest enemy of the one who loves holiness. Here sin makes war upon you as the flesh lusts against the Spirit (Galatians 5:17). As the hymnwriter asks: Would you be free from your burden of sin? Bunyan's Pilgrim fled the city of destruction seeking relief from the great burden of sin which he carried about with him. Heaven is the place where sin will be no more. This is pictured beautifully in Revelation 21:3-4: "And God Himself shall be among them, and He shall wipe away every tear from their eyes; and there shall no longer be any death; there shall no longer be any mourning, or crying, or pain; the first things have passed away." Why are there tears? Why is there death? Why do men mourn, cry, and feel pain? It is all because of sin. Sin brings all of those evils upon man. In heaven men shall be free from sin.

Second, in heaven men shall be free from the causes of sin. There are three primary causes of sin: your sinful nature, the temptations of the devil, and the lure of the world. Your sinful nature is the source of the sins which you commit. James tells us: "Each one is tempted when he is carried away and enticed by his own lust. Then when lust has conceived it gives birth to sin" (James 1:14-15). Your sinful nature spews out poison, filth, and vileness every day of your life in this world. If the devil were chained up and not allowed to touch or tempt you, you would continue to sin because of the principle of sin which indwells you: "For I know that nothing good dwells in me, that is in my flesh" (Romans 7:18). In heaven your vile body shall be made like unto His glorious body and you cannot sin.

In heaven you will be free from the temptations of the devil. Here men are assaulted daily by the enemy of their souls. Here "your adversary, the devil, prowls about like a roaring lion, seeking someone to devour" (I Peter 5:8). On earth the devil seeks to sift you as wheat as he sought to do to Peter. Soon the devil shall be thrown into the lake of fire and be tormented day and night forever and ever (Revelation 20:10). Soon, if you are a true believer in Jesus Christ, "the God of peace will crush Satan under your feet" (Romans 16:20). In heaven there shall be no more devil to tempt saints to sin anymore.

In heaven men shall be free from the lusts of the world. These are described by John as "the lusts of the flesh and the lust of the eyes and the boastful pride of life" (I John 2:16). Here the world system seeks to press you into it's mold. Christians are constantly being bombarded by the ungodly influences of lust, greed, pride, etc. These ungodly influences working hand-in-hand with your corrupt nature bring much grief to your soul. In heaven the godly shall be free of the evil influence of the world for they will have overcome the world for all time through the blood of Jesus Christ.

Finally, in heaven men will be free from the consequences of sin. The primary consequence of sin is eternal punishment in hell. Scripture makes it clear that a person at death goes to either heaven or hell. There is no in between state or place, no purgatory, no other option. Those who go to heaven are spared the wrath of God which falls upon those in hell. They are delivered from "the wrath to come" (I Thessalonians 1:10). Physical death which opens the door into eternity is also one of the consequences of sin. Death came originally, as a direct penal infliction upon man because of his sin for "the sting of death is sin" (I Corinthians 15:56), "but thanks be to God, who gives us the victory through our Lord Jesus Christ. Death is swallowed up in victory" so that the child of God can boldly say, "Oh, death where is your victory? O death, where is your sting?" (I Corinthians 15:54, 55, & 57).

We shall now look at what the eternal blessedness of the soul consists of in heaven. Paul said, "Now we see through a glass darkly" (I Corinthians 13:12). Certainly, the picture we now try to describe is dark indeed compared to the true glory of heaven. Who can imagine the things we now try to describe? "We shall never understand glory fully till we are in heaven. Let me give you some dark views only, some imperfect lineaments of that state of glory at which the saints shall arrive after death."[3] The blessedness of the soul in glory consists of at least three things: 1) the seeing of God, 2) the perfection of graces in the believer, and 3) fulness of joy.

"Blessed are the pure in heart, for they shall see God" (Matthew 5:8). The saints in heaven shall see God in all His majesty. They shall behold the infinite glory of the Almighty One in as great a capacity as they are capable of. They shall not behold Him only at a distance, but "face to face" (I Corinthians 13:12). This is what the blessedness of the saints in glory chiefly consists of: the beholding of God. Yet it is impossible that a finite man should comprehend God. Revelation 22:5 describes some of the glory of seeing God: "And there shall no longer be any night; and they shall not have need of the light of a lamp nor the light of the sun, because the Lord God shall illumine them." The glory of God will swallow up the light of the sun as the brilliance of the sun now dispels the darkness of night.

The Father will not directly manifest Himself to those in heaven for we are told in the Scriptures that God is invisible: "Now to the King eternal, immortal, *invisible,* the only God, be honor and glory forever and ever. Amen" (I Timothy 1:17). It is said of Christ that "He is the image of the *invisible* God" (Colossians 1:15). The Father will not need to manifest Himself in any other way than through the glory and majesty of the exalted Christ. The Lord told His disciples on the night before He died: "He who has seen Me has seen the Father" (John 14:9). Jonathan Edwards described the believer's seeing Christ in glory this way: "The seeing God in the glorified body of Christ, is the most perfect way of seeing God with the bodily eyes that can be; for in seeing a real body, which one of the Persons of the Trinity has assumed to be His body, and in which He dwells forever as his own, the divine majesty and excellency appear as much as it is possible for them to appear in outward form or shape...They shall see Him, as appearing in His glorified human nature, with their bodily eyes; and this will be a most glorious sight. The loveliness of Christ as thus appearing will be a most ravishing thing to them; for though the bodies of the saints shall appear with an exceeding beauty and glory, yet the body of Christ will without doubt immensely surpass them, as much as the brightness of the sun does that of the stars. The glorified body of Christ will be the masterpiece of all God's workmanship in the whole material universe. There shall be in his glorious countenance the manifestations of His glorious spiritual perfections, His majesty, His holiness, His surpassing grace, and love, and meekness. The eye will never be wearied with beholding this glorious sight."[4]

Not only will they see Christ face to face, but they will walk with Him and talk with Him. Christ shall treat them as brothers and shall speak to them as His intimate friends. Just before His crucifixion, Christ told His disciples: "No longer do I call you slaves, for a slave does not know what his master is doing; but I have called you friends, for all things that I have heard from My Father I have made known to you" (John 15:15). If Christ could say this to His disciples while they were still clothed in their sinful natures, do you think He will not admit them nearer to Him in heaven when they have been fully purged of all stain and iniquity and stand before His throne spotless clothed in His blood? Certainly he will. The Scriptures speak of God's living with and among His people in glorious terms: "Behold the tabernacle of God is among men, and He shall dwell among them, and they shall be His people, and God Himself shall be among them...and they shall see His face, and His name shall be on their foreheads" (Revelation 21:3

& 22:4).

Secondly, those who are admitted to heaven shall enjoy the perfection of all their graces. We shall look at three graces particularly: 1) the grace of knowledge, 2) the grace of holiness, and 3) the grace of love. First, the grace of knowledge shall be perfected in glory. "For now we know in part, and prophesy in part; but when the perfect comes, the partial will be done away...For now we see in a mirror dimly, but then face to face; now I know in part, but then I shall know fully just as I also have been fully known" (I Corinthians 13:9-10 & 12). Now our knowledge of divine things is shallow and indistinct. We do not perceive things clearly. We are sluggish in our understandings. Then we shall know, as Christ now knows us. The grace of knowledge shall be perfected in the godly in heaven. The godly shall understand more fully Christ as Mediator between God and men. They shall understand the mystery of the incarnation, of God becoming man. To as great a degree as possible, those in glory shall understand the mystery of the Trinity. They shall understand the plan of salvation and how divine providence worked in all the circumstances of their lives. There all the difficulties, trials, and dark providences of life shall be seen as a glorious entity which will testify to the truth that "all things work together for good to those who love God" (Romans 8:28). They shall understand the excellencies of Christ to as full a degree as they are capable. The knowledge of God shall be full, yet God shall not be fully known, for man can never completely comprehend the Godhead.

The grace of holiness shall be perfected in all who are received into glory. "We know that when He appears, we shall be like Him" (I John 3:2). Holiness is the transcendent beauty of God and the angels. Holiness is primary among the attributes of God. "Holy, holy, holy is the Lord of hosts" (Isaiah 6:3) is the cry of the seraphim who constantly attend Him in glory. In heaven holiness will be perfected in the believer. Sin shall be no more. Then the words of God shall fully be brought to pass: "You shall be holy, for I am holy" (I Peter 1:16). Holiness is the fervent desire of the saint as he travels through this world of sin. There the saints shall be as the angels of God. There, as much as can be, they shall be like Christ Himself. They shall be holy.

In heaven the grace of love shall be perfected. On earth love to God is expressed in fits and spasms. Sinful flesh and self-interest dampen and hinder love to God. We cannot love God as we ought or even as we would like to. Although the spirit in the child of God desires with all that is within him to do what the Scripture says, to "Love the Lord your God with all your heart and with all your soul and with all your might" (Deuteronomy 6:5), it cannot be done perfectly here. But as he in his heart desires to do so, God accepts the desire in the believer as if the action were done perfectly. In heaven, unhindered love shall flow forth to God as none have ever experienced on earth. God shall be loved completely and fully and the saints shall love one another without carnality or selfishness being present.

Thirdly, those who are in heaven shall experience fulness of joy. "In Thy presence is fulness of joy; in Thy right hand are pleasures forever" (Psalm 16:11). Fulness of joy could be described as experiencing the bountiful love of God to them as the waters of an ocean. Others, who have a far greater understanding of this than I do, have described it in this way: "From this glorious manifestation of God's love will flow infinite joy into the souls of the blessed; therefore heaven is called 'entering into the joy of our Lord' (Matthew 25:21). The seeing of God, loving God, and being beloved of God will cause a jubilation of spirit, and create such holy raptures of joy in the saints, that are unspeakable and full of glory."[5] "They shall see in Him all that love desires. Love desires the love of the beloved. So the saints in glory shall see God's transcendent love to them; God will make ineffable manifestations of His love to them. They shall see as much love in God towards them as they desire; they neither will nor can crave any more...When they see God so glorious, and at the same time see how greatly God loves them, what delight will it not cause in the soul! Love desires union. They shall therefore see this glorious God united to them, and see themselves united to Him. They shall see that He is their Father, and that they are His children. They shall see God gloriously present with them; God with them; and God in them; and they in God. Love desires the possession of its object. Therefore they shall see God, even their own God; when they behold this transcendent glory of God, they shall see Him as their own."[6] The one in glory shall enjoy God as far as their capacity allows.

The Psalmist wrote of the great blessing attending the worship of God in His temple: "How blessed are those who dwell in Thy house! They are ever praising Thee...For the Lord God is a sun and shield; the Lord gives grace and glory; no good thing does He withhold from those who walk uprightly" (Psalm 84:4 & 11). Those in heaven shall rightly say: "How blessed are those who stand in Thy very presence!" If the Lord withholds nothing on earth from those who walk uprightly, shall He then withhold any of the glory of heaven from His redeemed?

Here we enjoy God primarily through His Word, ordinances of worship, and prayer. There we shall enjoy Him "face to face." "Here you have God in expectation, but there you shall have Him in possession."[7] There the saints in glory shall be filled with joy through the eternal enjoyment of the manifestation of God in all His attributes. It will greatly add to the joy and rejoicing of those in glory when they contemplate God's mercy shown to them in salvation and how they deserved to be among the damned, but were spared the torments of hell solely because of God's sovereign mercy given to them. Ministers will rejoice with those whom they led to the knowledge of Christ and the fruits of their labors will be fully seen there. Paul writes of this joy in I Thessalonians 2:19: "For who is our hope or joy or crown of exultation? Is it not even you, in the presence of our Lord Jesus at His coming?" Other things will undoubtedly contribute to their joy, such as their being with loved ones and the saints of all the ages, the contemplating of God's providences toward them on earth, being in the heavenly city, but the greatest joy of all will come from being in His presence!

QUESTIONS ANSWERED

Both Christians and non-Christians often have questions about life after death and very often the questions are the same ones. In this section we shall look at several common questions people ask about heaven. We shall explore these issues: 1) What happens when a Christian dies? 2) Will those in heaven know each other? 3) Will those in heaven sorrow over loved ones who are in hell? And 4) Are there different degrees of glory and rewards in heaven?

What happens when a Christian dies? Does he go to heaven immediately upon death or does he lie in the grave in a state of soul sleep awaiting the resurrection? Is he conscious or unconscious?

Christ and the Scriptures give us a clear answer to this question. In Luke 16 the Lord Jesus tells us of two men who died, one was ungodly and the other was a godly man named Lazarus. Both were conscious immediately after death. Our purpose here is to inquire into what happened to Lazarus, the godly man, at the time of his physical death. Christ tells us: "Now it came about that the poor man (Lazarus) died and he was carried away by the angels to Abraham's bosom" (Luke 16:22). Angels met Lazarus upon his departure from this earthly life and carried him into glory. While Lazarus' body lay rotting in the grave, his soul was transported by the wings of holy angels into heaven. Christ confirms this very thing in his response to the thief on the cross when He told the thief: "Truly I say to you, today you shall be with Me in Paradise" (Luke 23:43). Some might doubt that the Paradise Christ referred to was really heaven; however, Paul uses the same word to describe the third heaven saying that he "was caught up into Paradise, and heard inexpressible words, which a man is not permitted to speak" (II Corinthians 12:4). The true follower of Christ goes to be with Christ in heaven immediately after death.

Paul speaks of this issue in several places. One is found in Philippians 1:21-23: "For me to live is Christ, and to die is gain. But if I am to live on in the flesh, this will mean fruitful labor for me; and I do not know which to choose. But I am hard-pressed in both directions, having the desire to depart and be with Christ, for that is very much better." And in a similar passage: "Therefore, being always of good courage, and knowing that while we are at home in the body we are absent from the Lord...we are of good courage, I say, and prefer to be absent from the body and to be at home with the Lord" (II Corinthians 5:6 & 8). Several observations can be made from these Scriptures. The first is that Paul considered dying to be gain to him. How could this be true if all death meant was that he would lie in a grave unconscious and rot for thousands of years? Paul also tells us that when he departed this life he would go to be with Christ and that to do so was "very much better" than continuing to live here. In II Corinthians, Paul contrasts living in the body and therefore being apart from Christ, with dying (being absent from the body) and being with Christ. For Paul, and all true godly persons, death means that the soul goes to be with Christ, carried there by holy angels while the physical body lies in the grave to await the resurrection and the reuniting of soul and body. Oh, how this should comfort the godly who are ill and near death! How this should be of great assurance to those godly ones who may now have a fear of death. Death brings a glorious transition to the believer. Death ushers him into the presence of Christ and glory! Oh, then you who are godly, do not fear death as an enemy, but be willing to welcome it as a friend when your appointed time comes. Death is the key that unlocks the door to everlasting happiness for the saint.

Will those in heaven recognize their friends, relations, and those they knew on earth there? Shall believers not know anyone when they get to glory? Shall the godly know all those in glory or just those whom they knew on earth?

Let me answer first from inference. If the damned in hell were to be shown to recognize the godly in heaven, then would you not think that the godly should at least know each other there? Let us look again at Luke 16:22-24: "And the rich man died and was buried. And in Hades he lifted up his eyes, being in torment, and saw Abraham far away, and Lazarus in his bosom. And he cried out, 'Father Abraham, have mercy on me, and send Lazarus...'" Dives, the rich man in hell, recognized Lazarus, whom he knew in his lifetime, and also Abraham, whom he had never seen or met. Certainly, the glorified saints in heaven know as much as the damned in hell do, don't they? By inference we conclude that the godly do know each other in heaven.

When Christ stood on the mount of transfiguration Moses and Elijah appeared with Him and were immediately recognized by Peter: "And Elijah appeared to them along with Moses; and they were conversing with Jesus. And Peter answered and said to Jesus, 'Rabbi, it is good for us to be here; and let us make three tabernacles, one for You, and one for Moses, and one for Elijah'" (Mark 9:4-5). If Peter and the apostles knew glorified saints in heaven when they were yet mortal and on the earth, then much more so will the godly recognize their friends and even those whom they never knew on earth when they come to glory; for Abraham also recognized Dives, a man in hell, whom he had never met on earth and Abraham even knew details of his life (Luke 16:25-26). Christ speaks of the damned on judgment day weeping when they "see Abraham and Isaac and Jacob and all the prophets in the kingdom of God, but yourselves being cast out" (Luke 13:28).

Thus we have abundant evidence that the glorified saints will know not only their earthly acquaintances, but will know all those in glory as soon as they arrive there. If you are godly, you shall see Moses, and know him, and he will know you; you shall see Paul, Noah, Peter, the prophets and the apostles and know them, and they shall know you. Husband and wife shall know each other. Sons and daughters shall see their fathers and mothers. Ministers shall see those whom they led to Christ on earth. This will greatly heighten the joy of saints as they rejoice forever with all the saints of all the ages. What a wonderful day that will be for the godly!

Will those in heaven sorrow and weep for persons whom they knew and loved in this world who are being tormented in hell? We have already established that those in heaven both see and recognize those in hell. Both Abraham and Lazarus knew Dives and were able to see him being tormented in hell. That hell is visible from the gates of heaven is confirmed in Isaiah 66:23-24: "'All mankind will come to bow down before Me' says the Lord. 'Then they shall go forth and look on the corpses of the men who have transgressed against Me. For their worm shall not die and their fire shall not be quenched; and they shall be an abhorrence to all mankind.'" Those in hell are said to be an abhorrence to all those who worship God in heaven. This may seem strange at first until we probe into why this is.

Revelation 16:5-7 gives us a look into the portals of heaven as we see angels and glorified saints praising God for His judgment of the wicked on earth: "And I heard the angel of the waters saying, 'Righteous art Thou who art and who wast, O Holy One, because Thou didst judge these things; for they poured out the blood of saints and prophets, and Thou hast given them blood to drink. They deserve it.' And I heard the altar saying, 'Yes, O Lord God, the Almighty, true and righteous are Thy judgments.'" Angels and saints in heaven rejoice in the punishment of the wicked, not because it is punishment for punishment's sake, but because it is perfectly just and righteous punishment, fully deserved by those who are suffering it. They will delight in seeing the justice and power of God glorified in this manner.

The saints in heaven have a far greater concern for the glory of God than the most zealous believer on earth. Jonathan Edwards spoke of the reaction of the saints in glory to the sufferings of the wicked in hell in his sermon *The End of the Wicked Contemplated by the Righteous:* "The saints in glory will see how the damned are tormented; they will see God's threatenings fulfilled, and His wrath executed upon them. When they see it, it will be no occasion of grief to them...It will be an occasion of their rejoicing, as the glory of God will appear in it. The glory of God appears in all His works: and therefore there is no work of God which the saints in glory shall behold and contemplate, but what will be an occasion of rejoicing to them. God glorifies Himself in the eternal damnation of the ungodly men...The saints in heaven will be perfect in their love to God: their hearts will be a flame of love to God, and therefore they will greatly value the glory of God, and will exceedingly delight in seeing Him glorified...They will therefore greatly rejoice in all that contributes to that glory. The glory of God will in their esteem be of greater consequence, than the welfare of thousands and millions of souls."[8]

Other Scriptures bear out this teaching: that those in heaven will, in fact, rejoice at the just sufferings of the damned: "Rejoice over her, O heaven, and you saints and apostles and prophets, because God has pronounced judgment for you against her" (Revelation 18:20). "'Hallelujah! Salvation and glory and power belong to our God; because His judgments are true and righteous; for he has judged the great harlot who was corrupting the earth with her immorality, and has avenged the blood of His bondservants on her.' And a second time they said, 'Hallelujah! Her smoke rises up forever and ever'" (Revelation 19:1-3). Likewise Moses rejoiced and sang God's praises when he saw God's glory manifested in the destruction of Pharaoh and all his forces (Exodus 15:1-12) and Proverbs 21:15 tells us: "The execution of justice is joy for the righteous."

It is not from a lack of love that the saints in heaven will rejoice at the punishment of the wicked, but because their love has been perfected and they now see things just as God does. They will then hate sin with a perfect hatred and see the absolute vileness of the practitioners of sin who rejected the councils of God and they will abhor them. Saints in heaven love what God loves and hate what God hates. Edwards continues: "However the saints in heaven may have loved the damned while here, especially those of them who were near and dear to them in this world, they will have no love for them hereafter."[9]

Christians here on earth are to love, pray for, and seek the salvation of all because there exists the possibility that even the most wicked man might receive the grace of God and be saved. In eternity no such possibility exists. The ungodly there are in the same condition as the demons are here: unredeemable and beyond hope. Do you weep oceans of tears for demons now? Do you pray fervently that they might be saved? Why not? Is it not because they are thoroughly evil and beyond all hope of salvation? So it is with the ungodly there. There the Scripture will be fulfilled which says, "Let the one who does wrong, still do wrong; and let the one who is filthy, still be filthy" (Revelation 22:11). There the ungodly will be seen by the saints through holy eyes for what they are and will be for all eternity: wrongdoers, filthy, vile, haters of God. And through holy eyes "a reprobate is despised" (Psalm 15:4).

Are there different degrees of glory in heaven? Do those who labor more for God's kingdom and glory here on earth receive a greater degree of honor and glory there? If so, will this not cause problems as it does here?

The first evidence we have of different degrees of glory comes from what is sometimes called the law of contraries. Are there different degrees of torment in hell? If so, then, by the law of contraries, we could logically deduct that there will be different degrees of glory in heaven. In Luke 12:47-48 we are told of those who will "receive many lashes" and whose who "will receive but few." There are different degrees of punishment in hell, thus we conclude that likewise there will be different degrees of blessedness in heaven.

II Corinthians 5:10 and I Corinthians 3:8 tell us the basis for the difference: "For we must all stand before the judgment seat of Christ that each one may be recompensed for his deeds in the body, whether good or bad." "Each will receive his own reward according to his own labor." It is apparent that free rewards are promised to believers in glory which will be equivalent to what we have done in our labors for the Lord here on earth. The Scripture speaks of the one who receives "a prophet's reward" (Matthew 10:41) which seems to distinguish it as being different than the ordinary reward. Christ taught His disciples that whoever gave to them "a cup of water to drink" in His name would not lose his reward (Mark 9:41). This would not be possible if there were no recognition of good works in heaven.

Other Scriptures state quite clearly that a difference will be made between believers in glory. Daniel is told that "those who have insight will shine brightly like the brightness of the expanse of heaven, and those who lead many to righteousness, like the stars forever and ever" (Daniel 12:3). And Paul compares the difference between the sun, moon, and stars and applies it to believers in glory: "There is one glory of the sun, and another glory of the moon, and another glory of the stars; for star differs from star in glory. So also is the resurrection of the dead" (I Corinthians 15:41-42). Paul is saying that just as one star shines more brightly than another in the sky, so one saint shall shine with more heavenly glory than another when the dead are raised to receive the things done in the body. One shall be more glorious than another based on how they have lived, what they have done for Christ, while living on earth. This is plainly taught in the parable of the talents as well, where one man was put in authority over ten cities and another over five (Luke 19:12-19).

"The saints are like so many vessels of different sizes cast into a sea of happiness where every vessel is full: this is eternal life, for a man to have his capacity filled. But after all tis left to God's sovereign pleasure, tis His prerogative to determine the largeness of the vessel."[10] Each person will be filled to their capacity with blessedness and joy. None will lack anything. But there will be those who have a greater capacity for joy than others. Christopher Love explains: "Though there be degrees of glory, yet this doth not imply, that there shall be defects or want (lack) of glory in heaven to any glorified persons, but every person shall be as full of glory as he can hold, or is capable of. Perkins explains it by a clear demonstration. Take a little vessel and a great vessel, and cast both these into the sea, both these vessels will be full, yet there is not in the little vessel as in the great, though both are full. So, saith he, the godly are like two vessels, yet one, by reason of the enjoyment of God, is more capacious (spacious) to take in more of God than the other is, yet the least saint shall be full of glory; he that hath least glory, shall have glory sufficient, though not glory equal with some glorified saints: so that degrees of glory doth not argue any defect in those persons that have less glory than others have."[11] Jonathan Edwards believed that the degree of glory or reward would be determined by four factors: degrees of grace and holiness here, degree of good that is done, self-denial and suffering, and eminency in humility.[12] All will be filled vessels, but of different sizes. All shall wear crowns, some with a greater luster than others. Holiness and happiness shall be greater in some than in others throughout all eternity.

The presence of different degrees of glory in heaven does not mean that such a thing as envy will exist in heaven. All love will be perfected in heaven and thus it will be as the Apostle wrote: "If one member is honored, all members rejoice with it" (I Corinthians 12:26). The saints in glory will think it is right that those who excelled others in works of righteousness and bringing glory to God on earth should receive greater glory in heaven. Men will bless God for the radiance of His glory shining through other men, for envy and sin will have no part in His kingdom.

I will offer only limited application of this here and more fully apply it in the next section. Believers, your eternal state rests upon what you do here on earth. "Now this I say, he who sows sparingly, shall also reap sparingly; and he who sows bountifully shall also reap bountifully" (II Corinthians 9:6). Would you seek the best eternity possible? Then live your life fully for God's glory today. Tomorrow may be too late. Your present life will determine your future state of glory, but more on this later.

APPLICATION TO BELIEVERS AND UNBELIEVERS

"And a highway will be there, a roadway, and it will be called 'the highway of holiness.' The unclean will not travel on it, but it will be for him who walks that way, and fools will not wander on it" (Isaiah 35:8). One of the fears I have in writing of the glory of heaven is that there is a natural tendency for carnal men to apply a pleasing doctrine to themselves when they have no legitimate basis for doing so. Heaven is not to be obtained by the lazy and slothful, nor the unclean and profane, not even by those who are regular church attenders if they are not holy in their lives and practice. The highway to heaven is indeed "a highway of holiness" and it is for "him who walks that way," that is, for the one who lives a holy life. In a sermon preached by Jonathan Edwards in the early 1720's, Edwards noted: "If everyone that hoped for heaven got there, heaven by this time would have been full of murderers, adulterers, common swearers, drunkards, thieves, robbers, and licentious debachers."[13]

Christ said: "Blessed are the pure in heart, for they shall see God" (Matthew 5:8). Heaven is for the one whose heart is pure. Heaven is for the one who lives a holy life. Heaven is for the one who loves Jesus Christ more than all other people and all other things. "Tis therefore exceedingly absurd, and even ridiculous, for any to pretend they have

a good heart, while they live a wicked life, or don't bring forth the fruit
of universal holiness in their practice. For tis proved in fact, that such
men don't love God above all. Tis foolish to dispute against plain fact
and experience. Men that live in ways of sin, and yet flatter themselves
that they shall go to heaven, or expect to be received hereafter as holy
persons, without a holy life and practice, act as though they expected
to make a fool of their Judge."[14]

Do not assume that because you desire to go to heaven, that you will.
Be willing to strictly examine your heart to see if you have any sound
reason to hope for heaven. Ponder these questions in your heart: Were
you ever thoroughly convicted of your sinful heart and nature? Have
you seen yourself as vile in your own eyes? Do you live in the practice
of any hidden or secret sin? Do you hate all sin as sin? Which
dominates your affections, thoughts, and desires more: the world or
Jesus Christ? Do you love Christ more than father, mother, husband,
wife, son, or daughter? Do you love Jesus Christ for who He is or just
what He can do for you? Do you love a life of holiness and obedience
to the Word of God or is it burdensome to you? When you do good
things, do you do them to glorify God or so that men will praise and
love you for them? Do you really love God or do you just fear His
threats of judgment against you? Do not read over these questions
quickly and hurry on, but search your hearts with them. Many who
profess to be Christians today are simply outwardly religious, but their
hearts have never been changed by the regenerating power of the Spirit
of God.

Is heaven a glorious kingdom, a city of pure gold, a Paradise? Then
you who are unconverted or who are falsely persuaded of your good
condition do not lose this place for the bobbles, trifles, and trinkets of
the world! Nothing you can desire or acquire on earth compares with
the glory of heaven. Is heaven called Paradise? Will you forego
seeking a heavenly paradise for an earthly one? Would you rather lie
in the bed of Delilah and then drink from the fires of hell, or have your
eternal home by the throne of God and the Lamb and drink from the
river of the water of life? Did Christ say in His Father's house were
many mansions? Then do not waste all your time and money building
an earthly mansion for yourself. Your earthly house will not last. One
day it will be leveled to the ground. It is of no eternal value. A house
in heaven is an everlasting habitation. Jesus Christ said, "Do not lay up
for yourselves treasures upon earth, where moth and rust destroy, and
where thieves break in and steal. But lay up for yourselves treasures in
heaven...for where your treasure is, there will your heart be" (Matthew
6:19-21). The pursuit of temporary lusts and pleasures on earth at the

expense of a heavenly kingdom is the act of a simpleton. Esau sold his inheritance for a bowl of chili. Do you think he made a good bargain? Your lips may say 'no,' but what does your life say?

Have you ever really meditated upon the brevity of life? Truly, we are here today and gone tomorrow. James expressed it this way: "Yet you do not know what your life will be like tomorrow. You are just a vapor that appears for a little while and then vanishes away" (James 4:14). Man's life is variously described in God's word as "a mere breath" (Psalm 39:5); "a flower of the field" (Psalm 103:15); "grass that withers" (James 1:11); "a shadow" (Job 14:2); and "a phantom" (Psalm 39:6). Everything in this life is uncertain. Riches may be lost in a day (Ecclesiastes 5:14). A man who seems to be robust and healthy one day may be stricken with sickness the next day (Job 2:7). Friends or close relatives may die (II Samuel 19:4). Why should you invest your life for that which is transcient and passing away? Most today live as if earth is the only heaven there is. "Their inner thought is, that their houses are forever" (Psalm 49:11). But hear the Word of God: "But man in his pomp will not endure...For when he dies he will carry nothing away; his glory will not descend after him. Though while he lives he congratulates himself" (Psalm 49:12 & 17-18). Is it worth gambling away eternity for that which is temporary, uncertain, and passing away? Heaven is a kingdom that endures forever; so does hell.

Finally, I would have you consider both your body and your soul. People spend countless hours decorating their faces and cleaning and perfuming their bodies. Vain persons spend thousands of dollars for face lifts and plastic surgery in an effort to appear more beautiful to themselves and other equally vain persons. Jesus Christ calls His followers to a different set of values: "Do not be anxious for your life, as to what you shall eat, or what you shall drink; nor your body, as to what you shall put on. Is not life more than food, and the body than clothing?" (Matthew 6:25). Your soul is far more valuable than your body. Your body will die and rot in the grave. Your soul will live forever. "What is a man profited, if he gain the whole world, and lose his own soul?" (Matthew 16:26). How much time do you spend taking care of your body? How much time do you invest in seeking eternal life for your soul? Which is most important? Men will risk the destruction of their bodies and their lives to fight to obtain an earthly kingdom. Is not a heavenly kingdom worth much more?

The presence of different degrees of glory in heaven should stir up within the godly the desire to strive more diligently to bring greater glory to God on earth. The more holy violence we put forth in the exercise of duty here, the greater will be our glory there. Paul uses this very example in I Corinthians 9:24: "Do you not know that those who run in a race all run, but only one receives the prize? Run in such a way that you may win." Jonathan Edwards believed that ministers need not apologize for an appeal to good works on the basis of rewards and stated, "Persons need not and ought not to set any bounds to their spiritual and gracious appetites...We ought to seek high degrees of glory in heaven."[15] Thomas Watson agreed, writing: "Consider then seriously, the more violent we are for heaven and the more work we do for God, the greater will be our reward. The hotter our zeal, the brighter our crown. Could we hear the blessed souls departed speaking to us from heaven, surely they would say, 'Were we to leave heaven awhile and to dwell on the earth again, we would do God a thousand times more service than we have ever done; we would pray with more life, act with more zeal; for now we see that the more we have labored, the more astonishing is our joy and the more flourishing our crown.'"[16] Moses is said by the writer of Hebrews to have considered "the reproach of Christ greater riches than the treasures of Egypt; for he was looking to the reward" (Hebrews 11:26). Solomon exhorts the people to "Cast your bread on the surface of the waters, for you will find it after many days" (Eccelsiastes 11:1). And Paul reminds us "he who sows bountifully shall reap bountifully" (II Corinthians 9:6). Seek then to lay up greater treasures in heaven by your zealousness for God's glory on earth.

By way of general application I will mention several things briefly. It is of utmost importance that those who believe they are God's children should labor for a true scripturally-grounded assurance that they are, in fact, heirs of heaven. Do not expect to be among the glorified in heaven, if you have brought no glory to Jesus Christ here on earth. "Every tree that does not bear good fruit is cut down and thrown into the fire" (Matthew 7:19). Peter admonishes men to "be all the more diligent to make certain about His calling and choosing you" (II Peter 1:10). Remember, Christ Jesus has said that "few" are those who find the kingdom of heaven. Are you sure you are numbered among those "few" who will be in heaven? Salvation is a much rarer work than is generally imagined.

For those who have lost friends or relatives who were godly do not grieve excessively for them. Paul wrote this message of encourage-ment to the Thessalonians who were concerned about the state of their departed loved ones: "But we do not want you to be uninformed, brethren, about those who are asleep, that you may not grieve, as do the rest who have no hope. For if we believe that Jesus died and rose again, even so God will bring with Him those who have fallen asleep in

Jesus...Therefore comfort one another with these words." (I Thessalonians 4:13-14 & 18). The doctrine of heaven should also help support the godly as they face death themselves. This world is the worst place you will ever live in, if you are Christ's. Death is a passageway into glory for the believer. Death is the end of all suffering, evil, sin, and pain. Death means that "we shall see Him as He is" (I John 3:2).

The doctrine of heaven should be an encouragement to believers to abstain from sin. Far from encouraging loose living among believers, a proper understanding of the doctrine of heaven with its rewards and degrees of glory should motivate them to stop sinning on earth. "Therefore do not let sin reign in your mortal bodies that you should obey its lusts" (Romans 6:12). Do not let your bodies be instruments of dishonor to God. "O Beloved, you shall see God with these very eyes you have now in your heads. You that are the elect of God, you shall sing Hallelujahs in heaven with this very tongue with which you converse among men. You shall lift up your hands in praises to God: Do not now use them, in the Apostle's phrase, as the weapons of unrighteousness to war against heaven. Do not use your eyes to be windows to lust, and your tongue to be tipped with frothy discourse, your hands to deceive, and your feet swift to shed blood. O do not use the members of your bodies, that are to be glorified with Jesus Christ in such sinful practices as these are."[17]

The doctrine of heaven should be of great comfort to those who are weary, suffering, or enduring persecution in this life. Christian, now you are nearer to your journey's end than when you first began. The time you have left on earth is miniscule when measured by eternity. The Hebrew Christians were reminded of their former victories in the time of trial and encouraged not to throw away their faith in the midst of present sufferings, "knowing that you have for yourselves a better possession and an abiding one" in heaven (Hebrews 10:34). Peter wrote to persecuted believers: "If you are reviled for the name of Christ, you are blessed, because the Spirit of glory and God rests upon you" (I Peter 4:14). In the time in which we live those who stand boldly for the truth will be ridiculed and slandered even by those who profess to be godly. Jesus Christ had special words for such as these: "Blessed are you when men revile you, and persecute you, and say all kinds of evil against you falsely, on account of Me. Rejoice, and be glad, for your reward in heaven is great, for so they persecuted the prophets who were before you" (Matthew 5:11-12). He who unjustly stains your name upon earth, unwillingly adds to your reward in heaven.

Finally the glory of heaven should make you extremely zealous for the conversion of souls while you are here. Do you wish to be with your as yet unconverted friends, relatives, and acquaintances in glory? Then labor with all your might for their conversion. Do not be selfish with your time, seeking after your own happiness, you are called to arms, to battle against the devil and all his forces, taking the gospel to the ends of the earth. Seek diligently the eternal welfare of others! "How shall they call upon Him in whom they have not believed? And how shall they believe in whom they have not heard? And how shall they hear without a preacher?" (Romans 10:14). Remember the words spoken to Daniel: "And those who have insight will shine brightly like the brightness of the expanse of heaven, and those who lead many to righteousness, like the stars forever and ever" (Daniel 12:3). They will shine brightly like the stars, forever and ever.

"How shall we escape if we neglect so great a salvation?"
(Hebrews 2:3).

[1] Paraphrased from Gregory's Morals quoted by Christopher Love, *Heaven's Glory, Hell's Terrors,* (London: John Rothwell, 1655), p. 87.

[2] Christopher Love, *Heaven's Glory, Hell's Terrors,* (London: John Rothwell, 1655), p. 101.

[3] Thomas Watson, *Body of Divinity,* (Grand Rapids: Baker Book House, 1979), p. 209.

[4] Jonathan Edwards, *The Works of Jonathan Edwards, Volume 2,* (Edinburgh: Banner of Truth, 1974), pp. 899 & 900.

[5] Thomas Watson, *Body of Divinity,* (Grand Rapids: Baker Book House, 1979), p. 210.

[6] Jonathan Edwards, *The Works of Jonathan Edwards, Volume 2,* (Edinburgh: Banner of Truth, 1974), p. 901.

[7] Christopher Love, *Heaven's Glory, Hell's Terrors,* (London: John Rothwell, 1655), p. 93.

[8] Jonathan Edwards, *The Works of Jonathan Edwards, Volume 2,* (Edinburgh: Banner of Truth, 1974), p. 208-209.

[9] Ibid, p. 209.

[10] Jonathan Edwards quoted by John Gerstner, *Heaven & Hell,* (Grand Rapids: Baker Book House, 1980), pp. 21-22.

[11] Christopher Love, *Heaven's Glory, Hell's Terrors,* (London: John Rothwell, 1655), p. 99.

[12] Jonathan Edwards quoted by John Gerstner, *Heaven & Hell,* (Grand Rapids: Baker Book House, 1980), p. 22.

[13] Ibid, p. 10.

[14] Jonathan Edwards, *Religious Affections,* (Binghamton, NY: Yale University Press, 1959), p. 426.

[15] Jonathan Edwards quoted by John Gerstner, *Heaven & Hell,* (Grand Rapids: Baker Book House, 1980), pp. 23.

[16] Thomas Watson, *Heaven Taken By Storm,* (Ligonier, PA: Soli Deo Gloria, 1992), pp. 78-79.

[17] Christopher Love, *Heaven's Glory, Hell's Terrors,* (London: John Rothwell, 1655), p. 118.

2

The Terrors of Hell

"So it will be at the end of the age; the angels shall come forth, and take out the wicked from among the righteous, and will cast them into the furnace of fire; there shall be weeping and gnashing of teeth" (Matthew 13:49-50).

The doctrine of hell is one of the most neglected doctrines in all of Scripture. When hell is mentioned today, it is generally ridiculed, as if the whole idea of hell were so old-fashioned that only the naive and ignorant would really believe that such a place actually exists. This is not hard to understand. Natural men hate the idea of being held accountable for their lives to a holy God, because they love sin and do not wish to part with it. The carnal mind throws up objection after objection to the idea of hell because it does not want to face the reality of it. Men live their lives thinking that maybe if they ignore a difficulty long enough that it will go away. Even conservative religious leaders are now attacking hell. Let men do what they will, the frivolous objections of the foolish will not do away with hell.

Amid the clamour to annihilate hell those who believe the Bible to be true must stand and speak. Your consideration of the terrors of hell may be one of the most important things you can do in this life. "Then he who hears the sound of the trumpet, and does not take warning, and a sword comes and takes him away, his blood will be on his own head" (Ezekiel 33:4). Please, I implore you, invest the time it takes to read this chapter and book to the end.

Why should one be so concerned about hell? Why should we spend time reading about hell? There are several reasons why it is profitable to do so:

1) Hearing of the terrors of hell may shock your consciences and awaken you out of your security.

2) Hearing about hell helps to deter men from committing sin. Both the godly and the ungodly are persuaded not to sin as much when they are regularly reminded of the terrors of hell.

3) Hearing about the terrors of hell may help to awaken those among you who may think they are saved because they believe in Christ or the facts of the gospel, but who are not really saved and are on their way to hell, but don't know it.

4) Preaching the doctrine of hell is profitable to both the godly and the

ungodly alike, as will be demonstrated.

Why aren't people fearful of hell? There seems to be a real lack of fear today of the reality of hell. This applies to both those who are in the church and those who are in the world. People are not afraid of hell. Why?

A man will not be afraid of a lion when it is only painted in a picture upon a wall. Why is this? Because it is only a picture. He knows that it is not real. But if you were left alone in a jungle and came face to face with a real lion that growled ferociously at you, you would be terrified. The consciences of men are much like the man who only views the painted lion. We hear of hell in the Bible. We know that the Lord Jesus spoke of hell. In fact, Christ spoke more of hell than anyone else in the Scriptures. Why do men not believe hell is real? Because they do not hear enough about it. We don't study what the Scriptures say about hell. It is not just what we hear which makes up what we believe, it is what we don't hear as well which helps to form our belief system. Only the Spirit of God can present the terrors of hell to our hearts in such a way as to see them alive before us. The doctrine of hell has been used by God more often to the conversion of sinners than any other doctrine in the Scriptures. Pray now that as you read this booklet the Holy Spirit might set hell before you as real indeed.

THE NECESSITY OF HELL

Most who scoff at hell today probably do so for several reasons. Primary among them is a desire to pursue their own paths of sin without having their consciences troubled about the consequences of their actions. They do not want to hear that what they are doing is wrong. They do not want to hear that their sin will be punished. I can hear someone say, "But isn't eternal torment in hell inconsistent with a merciful and loving God? How could a good God punish people in hell forever?" A misunderstanding of the character of God and the nature of sin can easily lead to such questions. Why is hell necessary? Let us examine several reasons for the necessity of hell.

1) The Great Evil in Sin & the Holiness of God. The difficulty most people have in understanding the necessity of hell is related to an incomplete and inadequate understanding of both how awful sin is and how glorious God is. We do not see what a great evil is in the least sin, nor do we understand God's holiness, His justice, and His wrath. If we saw sin as the greatest evil in the world and realized that every sin is a rejection of God's rule over us, a sneering at Him, a shaking of our fist in His face, and a hurling of dung at Him, we would begin to understand

a small bit of what our sin is like to God. Every time we sin, we either set ourselves, or a pet lust, up in our hearts as a rival god. Sin rejects the Creator as God and sets up the creature in His place.

If we could comprehend God's holiness and what it means to be holy, pure, perfect, upright, and untainted by the least sin, we would have a better idea of why God hates sin so much. Absolute holiness cannot tolerate the least sin, "Thine eyes are too pure to approve evil, and Thou canst not look on wickedness with favor" (Habakkuk 1:13). If we could understand the glorious holiness and purity of God and also the abominable nature of sin more, then we would have no problem with the absolute necessity of hell.

"The heart is more deceitful than all else and is desperately sick; who can understand it?" (Jeremiah 17:9). The human heart is sick. The human heart is wicked. The human heart is deceitful. The corruption in the heart causes us to be deceived about the awfulness of sin as well as many other things.

2) God's Infinite Nature. In understanding what our sin is really like, we must view it through the eyes of God. God is an infinite, eternal being. Every act of sin is committed against an infinite, holy God. In every act of sin we dethrone God and set ourselves above God. In every sin this question is the issue, "Whose will shall be done, God's will or man's? Now, man by sin sets his own will above the Lord's, and so kicks God as filth under his feet."[1] A single act of sin committed against a holy, infinite God deserves infinite punishment. It is an infinite evil to offend an infinite God even once.

3) Divine Justice. Even one sin against God calls for God to vindicate His name and His justice by punishing it as fully as it deserves. God can and will vindicate His justice. He promises to do so in Romans 12:19 where it says, "leave room for the wrath of God, for it is written, 'Vengence is mine, I will repay, says the Lord.'" One of the greatest preachers that ever lived, Jonathan Edwards, wrote, "The glory of God is the greatest good; it is that which is the chief end of creation; it is of greater importance than anything else. But this is one way wherein God will glorify Himself, as in the eternal destruction of ungodly men He will glorify His justice. Therein He will appear as a just governor of the world. The vindictive justice of God will appear strict, exact, awful, and terrible, and therefore glorious."[2]

A DESCRIPTION OF HELL

Hell is a furnace of unquenchable fire, a place of everlasting punishment, where its victims are tormented in both their bodies and their minds in accordance with their sinful natures, their actual sins committed, and the amount of spiritual light given to them, which they rejected. Hell is a place from which God's mercy and goodness have been withdrawn, where God's wrath is revealed as a terrifying, consuming fire, and men live with unfulfilled lusts and desires in torment forever and ever.

In Matthew 13:47-50 the Lord Jesus tells a parable relating to the judgment. In verses 49 & 50, the Lord describes the fate of the wicked: "So it will be at the end of the age; the angels shall come forth, and take out the wicked from among the righteous, and will cast them into the furnace of fire; there shall be weeping and gnashing of teeth."

In examining these words of the Lord Jesus we should first notice that hell is described as being a furnace of fire. Nebuchadnezzar's furnace was heated seven times hotter than normal and is described as "a furnace of blazing fire" (Daniel 3:23). John the Baptist spoke of "unquenchable fire" and Revelation describes hell as "a lake of fire burning with brimstone" (Revelation 19:20). Can we really imagine the horror of which these words speak? Imagine every part of your body on fire at the same time, so that every fiber of your being felt the intense torment of being burned. How long could you endure such punishment? Christ tells us that "there shall be wailing and gnashing of teeth." The lost will wail and gnash their teeth from having to endure the most intense pain and suffering they have ever felt as the flames consume them and constantly burn every part of their bodies. And there will be no relief.

Jonathan Edwards describes in graphic language what the fires of hell will be like: "Some of you have seen buildings on fire; imagine therefore with yourselves, what a poor hand you would make at fighting with the flames, if you were in the midst of so great and fierce a fire. You have often seen a spider or some other noisome insect, when thrown into the midst of a fierce fire, and have observed how immediately it yields to the force of the flames. There is no long struggle, no fighting against the fire, no strength exerted to oppose the heat, or to fly from it; but it immediately stretches forth and yields; and the fire takes possession of it, and at once it becomes full of fire. Here is a little image of what you will be in hell, except you repent and fly to Christ. To encourage yourselves that you will set yourselves to bear hell-torments as well as you can, is just as if a worm, that is about to be thrown into a glowing furnace, should swell and fortify itself, and prepare itself to fight the flames."[3]

Hell is also described as a place of darkness. The Lord tells us of the guest without wedding clothes who was cast "into outer darkness"

(Matthew 22:13). Jude writes of those in hell "for whom the black darkness has been reserved forever" (Jude 13). Christopher Love says in his work *Hell's Terrors:* "darkness is terrible, and men are more apt to fear in the dark then light: hell is therefore set forth in so terrible an expression, to make the hearts of men tremble; not only darkness, but the blackness of darkness".[4]

Hell is compared to Tophet in Isaiah 30:33. Tophet was the place where the idolatrous Jews sacrificed their children to the heathen god Molech by casting them into the fire. Day and night shrieks and howls were heard in that place, as day and night shrieks, howls, and wailing are heard in hell.

Isaiah speaks of "the breath of the Lord, like a stream of brimstone" setting hell ablaze. There is good evidence from the Scriptures that God Himself will be the fire in hell. Hebrews 12:29 says, "Our God is a consuming fire." The ungodly on earth ignorantly dance for joy when they hear pastors speak about the love and mercy of God, but they will be the beneficiaries of neither, unless they repent. To them God will be an all consuming fire. Hebrews 10:30-31 warns: "For we know him who said, 'Vengence is Mine, I will repay,' And again, 'The Lord will judge His people.' It is a terrifying thing to fall into the hands of the living God." It is a fearful thing, it is a terrible thing to fall into the hands of the living God! You shall not escape hell, sinner. God will be your hell and His wrath will consume you and be poured upon you as long as He exists. "Who understands the power of Thine anger?" (Psalm 90:11). It is because God Himself will be the fire in hell that words cannot possibly express the terrors of the damned in hell. "There is no reason to suspect that possibly ministers set forth this matter beyond what it really is, that possibly it is not so dreadful and terrible as it is pretended, and that ministers strain the description of it beyond just bounds...We have rather reason to suppose that after we have said our utmost, all that we have said or thought is but a faint shadow of reality."[5]

In Luke 16:19-26 Christ tells us of two men. One of them was rich (he has traditionally been called Dives); the other man was poor (his name was Lazarus). Both men died. The poor man was carried by angels to heaven and the rich man went to hell. The rich man did not go to hell because he was rich, nor did the poor man go to heaven simply because he was poor. The Lord shows us through this contrast that our circumstances may change drastically when we pass from time into eternity. We are not to be fooled that just because God may not have dealt harshly with us here, that he will not do so after death. The eternal abiding place of both men resulted from the condition of their hearts before God while on earth. Lazarus was a true follower of God. Dives was not. We want to carefully note what the Scriptures tell us about Dives and his condition, for from that we may learn much about hell. Verses 23 & 24 indicate to us that Dives is "in torment." What does it mean to be "in torment?" This torment refers to both torment in body and torment in soul as well. As we have seen, men's bodies will be tormented in a furnace of fire. Every part of the body will feel the pain of that fire. Men with severe stomach pains can be in great agony from that alone, but this pain will be far greater. Death from cancer is sometimes said to cause extreme pain in the body, but the pain of hell will be far worse. If your body were afflicted with many different and painful diseases all at the same time, you still would not begin to approach the pain of the damned in hell.

Men's consciences shall be in torment in hell as well. Conscience is the worm that will not die which the Scriptures speak of (Mark 9:48; Isaiah 66:24). Dives is told to "remember that during your life." Men will be tormented with extreme pain, but they will also be tormented by their own memories. They will remember hearing of hell and scoffing at it. They will remember being warned and told to repent or told that accepting the blessings of heaven without submitting to Christ as Lord falls short of salvation, but they took no heed to those warnings. They will be tormented by seeing at a distance the glories of heaven (as Dives was able to do), and knowing that for all eternity they will be damned. They will be tormented by unfulfilled desires and unfulfilled lusts (Dives is not able to receive even a drop of water to cool his tongue). They will be tormented by the knowledge that they will never escape from hell (Dives is told that "neither can you pass to us"). They will be tormented by the cries, shrieks, and curses of the damned around them. The most extreme torments a man can experience on earth will be like flea bites compared to the torments of hell.

Jonathan Edwards speaks of men unable to find even a moment of relief in hell in his sermon on The Future Punishment of the Wicked: "Nor will they ever be able to find anything to relieve them in hell. They will never find any resting place there; any secret corner, which will be cooler than the rest, where they may have a little respite, a small abatement of the extremity of their torment. They never will be able to find any cooling stream or fountain, in any part of that world of torment; no, nor so much as a drop of water to cool their tongues. They will find no company to give them any comfort, or do them the least good. They will find no place, where they can remain, and rest, and take breath for one minute: for they will be tormented with fire and brimstone; and they will have no rest day nor night forever and ever."[6]

THE ETERNITY OF HELL

The most terrifying aspect of all about hell is its length or duration. Hell is eternal. Hell will last forever. Can you comprehend eternity? No mathimatical equation or formula can explain it. Your mind cannot conceive of eternity, but it is none the less real. This aspect of hell alone should cause men to cry out in repentance. It is not surprising that skeptics of all ages have attacked the eternal nature of hell, substituting doctrines like the annihilation of the wicked in its place. Let us look at the Scriptures to verify the eternal nature of hell and to try and understand eternity better. Then we will explore why hell must be eternal.

"And the devil who deceived them was thrown into the lake of fire and brimstone, where the beast and the false prophet are also; and they will be tormented day and night forever and ever" (Revelation 20:10). This verse clearly gives us the duration of hell. Hell is forever and ever. How could a stronger, more certain expression be used? If the Spirit of God wanted to communicate the eternal nature of hell to men what could communicate it better than the expression "forever and ever?" The Scripture has no higher expression which is used to denote eternity than "forever and ever" for it is the very phrase used to tell us of the eternal existence of God Himself, as in Revelation 4:9: "to him who sits on the throne, to Him who lives forever and ever." Does anyone doubt that God will live to all eternity? How then can you doubt that hell will not last to all eternity when the same expression is used for both?

"We can conceive but little of the matter; but to help your conception, imagine yourself to be cast into a fiery oven, or a great furnace, where your pain would be as much greater than that occasioned by accidentally touching a coal of fire, as the heat is greater. Imagine also that your body were to lie there for a quarter of an hour, full of fire, and all the while full of quick sense; what horror would you feel at the entrance of such a furnace! and how long would that quarter of an hour seem to you! And after you had endured it for one minute, how overbearing would it be to you to think that you had to endure the other fourteen! But what would be the effect on your soul, if you knew you must lie there enduring that torment to the full for twenty-four hours...for a whole year...for a thousand years! Oh, then, how would your hearts sink, if you knew, that you must bear it forever and ever! that there would be no end! that after millions of millions of ages, your torment would be no nearer to an end, and that you never, never should be delivered! But your torment in hell will be immensely greater than this illustration represents."[7]

Christ, describing the great day of judgment, tells of the separation of the wicked and the righteous using these words: "And these will go away into eternal punishment, but the righteous into eternal life" (Matthew 25:46). Is there anyone who would deny that heaven exists eternally? Will the lives of the blessed in heaven be brought to an end one day? Of course not. But the same Greek word is used here in this verse to speak of the eternal life of the righteous and the everlasting punishment of the wicked. Hell will last as long as heaven does.

In hell there will be different degrees of torment appointed to men as indicated by a number of Scriptures. Luke 12:47-48 says: "And that slave who knew his master's will and die not get ready or act in accord with his will, shall receive many lashes, but the one who did not know it, and committed deeds worthy of a flogging, will receive but few." Christ says in Matthew 11:24: "Nevertheless I say to you that it shall be more tolerable for the land of Sodom in the day of judgment, than for you." The verses in Matthew indicate that the people in Capernaum will receive a greater punishment on judgment day than those who had lived in Sodom. The verses in Luke speak of a differentiation in judgment based on the amount of light received: some will receive many stripes and others will receive few.

Those who commit greater sins than others or more sins than others will receive greater punishment in hell (John 19:11). Religious hypocrites, those who profess Christianity but are not real Christians, will be punished more severely than others (Matthew 23:14-15). The Lord said of Judas Iscariot, "It would have been good for that man if he had not been born" (Matthew 26:24). How could any of these things be said to be true if annihilation were what awaited men after death? The presence of different degrees of punishment only makes sense in light of the ability to sensibly feel the torment. Could it be said that it would have been better for Judas if he had never been born if annihilation was all that awaited him? Annihilation is like no punishment at all.

Each time the unbeliever sins he is adding to his torment in hell. The person who sins twice as much as another with similar light will receive twice as much punishment. Every day that sinners continue to live and breathe here on earth without repenting, they are adding to their torments in hell. Romans 2:5 tells us: "But because of your stubborness and unrepentant heart you are storing up wrath for yourself in the day of wrath and revelation of the righteous judgment of God." The Lord Jesus encouraged the righteous to lay up treasures in heaven rather than on earth. The wicked are increasing their future wrath and torment in hell every day by their continued sinning. They add to their punishment daily. In hell men will wish that they had never been born.

Charles Haddon Spurgeon said: "In hell there is no hope. They have not even the hope of dying—the hope of being annihilated. They are forever—forever—forever lost! On every chain in hell, there is written "forever". In the fires there, blaze out the words, "forever". Above their heads, they read, "forever". Their eyes are galled and their hearts are pained with the thought that it is "forever". Oh, if I could tell you tonight that hell would one day be burned out, and that those who were lost might be saved, there would be a jubilee in hell at the very thought of it. But it cannot be—it is "forever" they are cast into the outer darkness."[8]

Christopher Love uses an illustration to try and help us understand what eternity means: "Suppose all the mountains of the earth were mountains of sand, and many more mountains still added thereto, till they reached up to heaven, and a little bird should once in every thousand years take one (grain of) sand of this mountain, there would be an innumerable company of years pass over before that mass of sand would be consumed and taken away, and yet this time would have an end; and it would be happy for man, if hell were no longer than this time; but this is man's misery in hell, he shall be in no more hope of coming out after he hath been there millions of years, then he was when he was first cast in there; for his torments shall be to eternity, without end, because the God that damns him is eternal."[9]

Earlier we looked at the necessity of hell or why there must be a place like hell. Now we will look at why hell must not only exist, but why it must exist eternally. Why is it necessary that hell be eternal? There are several answers to this which we shall explore briefly.

The first reason we will look at is the one mentioned by Christopher Love in the passage just quoted. The God who damns men is an eternal God. "Ultimately the eternality of hell is based upon the nature of God."[10] Is God's Word eternal? Is God's nature eternal? The Scripture tells us: "Jesus Christ is the same yesterday and today, yes and forever" (Hebrews 13:8). "His righteousness endures forever" (Psalm 111:3). "The Word of the Lord abides forever" (I Peter 1:24). If God's Word is eternal, if God's righteousness is eternal, if God Himself is eternal, then why shouldn't His wrath be eternal as well? As eternally existent, all of God's attributes are eternal and immutable; therefore, hell, as an expression of God's wrath, must be eternal.

Hell must be eternal because God's justice could never be satisfied by the punishment of sinners no matter how long it lasts. Christ makes this clear when He speaks about settling with your accuser before you get to court, otherwise you shall be cast into prison and "I tell thee, thou shalt not depart thence, till thou hast paid the very last mite" (Luke

12:59). Man can do nothing to pay for his sins. No amount of punishment in hell, no matter how long, can ever atone for sins. It is impossible; therefore, hell must be eternal.

Thirdly, hell must be eternal because the Scriptures tell us that the worm which gnaws the conscience of men in hell never dies. "For their worm shall not die, and their fire shall not be quenched" (Isaiah 66:24). If the worm never dies, then those being tormented by the worm shall never die.

Lastly, hell will be eternal because men continue to sin in hell. They increase and compound their guilt there. Hell is a place where tormented men curse God, curse themselves, and scream and wail with blasphemous language at their fellow men around them. Wicked men will increase each other's torments as they accuse, blame, and condemn one another. Men will not repent in hell because the character of sinners does not change. They remain sinners still. Men will sin to eternity, therefore God will punish them eternally.

APPLICATION TO BELIEVERS AND UNBELIEVERS

The Old Testament prophets warn us repeatedly of the dangers of hell: "Who among us can dwell with everlasting burnings?" (Isaiah 33:14, KJV). "Who can stand before His indignation? And who can endure the burning of His anger? His wrath is poured out like fire" (Nahum 1:6). Sinner, are you so arrogant as to think you can bear the wrath of God poured out in full measure upon you? You may think that hell is not so hot and that you will be able to bear it quite well. If you believe that you are more than a fool. The terrors of hell cause the devils to tremble and are you so foolish as to be unmoved by them or make light of them?

Do not think that simply because you go to church, or believe in God, or believe intellectually in the truths of Christianity that you will escape hell. The majority of those who regularly attend churches every week all over the world, will go to hell. Thomas Shepard, pastor and founder of Harvard University, wrote: "Formal professors and carnal gospelers have a thing like faith, and like sorrow, and like true repentance, and like good desires, but yet they be but pictures; they deceive others and themselves too...most of them that live in the church shall perish."[11]

You who profess to be Christians, but do not read your Bible much and pray little: how shall you escape the damnation of hell? You who are not especially bothered by little sins or troubled by the vain and filthy thoughts which you have: are you ready to go to hell? You who think the kingdom of God consists in a verbal profession of Christ or intellectually believing that Jesus died for your sins, but who are not concerned with living a holy, godly life and give little or no thought to God during the week: are you prepared to endure the torments of hell, day and night, forever and ever? You had better be, because if these things are true of you, you are headed straight for hell, unless you repent. Do not delude yourself! Christianity does not consist in words, or pious statements, or mere intellectual belief, but in a new heart and a new life dedicated to not sinning and living for the glory of God. If your heart and life have not been changed by God, you are still in your sins. If you are living in known disobedience to the word of God and are unconcerned about it, you have no right to assume you are going to heaven: you are on your way to hell! Repent of all your sins and turn to Jesus Christ and surrender to Him as Lord. Listen to the words of Christ: "If your eye causes you to stumble, pluck it out, and throw it from you. It is better for you to enter life with one eye, than having two eyes, to be cast into the fiery hell" (Matthew 18:9). "Nothing short of the complete denying of self, the abandoning of the dearest idol, the forsaking of the most cherished sinful course—figuratively represented under the cutting off of a right hand and the plucking out of a right eye—is what He claims from every one who would have true communion with Him."[12] But remember, the difficulty involved in forsaking all for Christ is nothing compared to spending eternity in hell.

I do not believe anyone can be scared into heaven, but I do believe they can be scared away from hell, so that they might begin to seek God with all their hearts, and to beg Christ to have mercy on them. Men stand on the brink of the pit of hell and are ready to fall headlong into it and yet they are completely unaware they are in any danger. If hearing about hell can cause otherwise senseless men to consider eternal truths, then preaching about hell is valuable indeed. It is better to view hell now, while you are living, and be terrified by it, than to have to endure hell forever when you die.

I would not have you to be more afraid of hell than of sin. Sin is your real enemy. Sin is worse than hell because sin gave birth to hell. Would you be willing to go to hell for all eternity for the enjoyment of a little pleasure and lust here on earth? Flee from sin! Flee from living for self and self-pleasing to Jesus Christ. When you die it will be to late. All opportunity to repent ends at death.

This doctrine is useful to the godly as well as the ungodly. The doctrine of hell should stir up within the righteous a fear of God. A godly fear is useful in many ways. The one who has a fear of God in his heart has a greater respect for the commandments of God. He who truly fears God will not fear men and would rather displease men than God

(Isaiah 8:12-13). This doctrine should increase your faithfulness and joy in Christ that you have been delivered from the torments of hell and should likewise increase your love for Christ who endured the wrath of God upon the cross for you.

The doctrine of hell should stir up within you a fear of sin. It should cause us to fear even little sins and be careful to confess and forsake sins of the heart and thought life also. Let the doctrine of hell keep you from the practice of sin.

The doctrine of hell should help the godly to be patient under all outward, temporary afflictions which come to them. No matter how great your afflictions are in this world, they are far less than the torments of hell from which the Lord has freed the godly. You may have to undergo lessor torments while on earth, but remember they are only temporary and you have been freed from the greatest of all torments so you may rejoice even in a time of affliction.

This doctrine is useful to motivate you to tell others of the message of Christ. Eryl Davies wrote in his book The Wrath of God: "The eternity of hell's sufferings should make us the more zealous and eager to tell people of the only One who is able to rescue them. Do we shrink from declaring these solemn truths? Does the thought of hell displease us? Remember that God will be glorified even through the eternal sufferings of unbelievers in hell. His injured majesty will be vindicated...What is supreme in the purpose of God in the election and reprobation of men is His own glory, and hell also will glorify the justice, power, and wrath of God throughout eternity. In the meantime it is our responsibility to pray and work for the salvation of sinners before such awful punishment overtakes them."[13]

I cannot leave without one final word to those who think they are converted, but are not; and also, to those who know themselves to be unconverted. Can you conceive of eternity? Stop now and try to imagine being tormented unceasingly, forever, without end. Does this not terrify you? Never a chance for a moment's rest. Never a drop of water to cool your parched throat. Think again of how long eternity is. Try to imagine it: day and night, forever and ever, burned with fire like a spider in a furnace of flames. Shrieking, howling, wailing, cursing the day you were born, and being cursed by the devils and damned souls around you eternally. Remembering, forever remembering, how you were warned on earth and how you ignored those warnings: self-satisfied and self-deceived that all was well with your soul. Job's wife told him to curse God and die. Unless you repent and flee to Jesus Christ, who is your only hope, you shall curse God eternally and be tormented by Him in His presence in the awful fullness of His wrath,

and you shall never die. You shall never die. You shall **never** die!
Eternity is forever!

[1] Thomas Shepard, *The Works of Thomas Shepard, Volume 1,* (New York: AMS Press, 1967), p. 94.

[2] Jonathan Edwards, *The Works of Jonathan Edwards, Volume 2,* (Edinburgh: Banner of Truth, 1974) p. 87.

[3] Ibid, p. 82.

[4] Christopher Love, *Hell's Terrors,* (London: T. M., 1653), p. 19.

[5] Jonathan Edwards, *The Works of Jonathan Edwards, Volume 2,* (Edinburgh: Banner of Truth, 1974) p. 884.

[6] Ibid, p.80.

[7] Ibid, p. 81.

[8] Charles Haddon Spurgeon, *The New Park Street Pulpit, Volume 1,* (Grand Rapids: Baker Book House, 1990), p. 308.

[9] Christopher Love, *Hell's Terrors,* (London: T. M., 1653), pp. 54-55.

[10] John Gerstner, *Heaven and Hell,* (Grand Rapids: Baker Book House, 1991), p. 77.

[11] Thomas Shepard, *The Works of Thomas Shepard, Volume 1,* (New York: AMS Press, 1967), p. 58.

[12] A. W. Pink, *Studies in the Scriptures,* January 1932, p. 18.

[13] Eyrl Davies, *The Wrath of God,* (Mid Glamorgan, Wales: Evangelical Press of Wales, 1984), p. 59.

3

The Narrow Road that Leads to Life

*"The gate is small, and the way is narrow that leads to
life, and few are those who find it" (Matthew 7:14).*

Many people today are inquiring about God. Most people know only
a little about God and what they have heard causes them to have a
distorted picture of Him. Most people create a "god" to their own liking
and who exists only in their own imaginations. The consequences of
creating a god to our own liking are nothing short of eternity in hell. We
can be wrong about some things, but to be wrong about salvation is the
greatest error we can make. It is fatal to our eternal souls.

This chapter has been designed to help those who are interested to
come to a better understanding of who God is and to place before you
the demands God makes of those who would be His followers.
Entering heaven is not easy. Jesus said, "Strive to enter by the narrow
door; for many, I tell you, will seek to enter and will not be able" (Luke
13:24). It is vitally important that each person take Jesus' words
seriously.

The message of this chapter might be summarized as follows:

1. God is our Creator; therefore, we are responsible to Him—both to
follow Him and to obey Him.
2. God is holy; therefore, He hates all sin. God is righteous and just,
so He must punish sin.
3. All men are born with a corrupt heart that loves sin and hates God.
The corruption in each man's heart causes him to want to go his own
way, do his own thing, and break God's laws.
4. The Person of Jesus Christ is God's only answer to the problem of
sin.
5. It is costly to be a follower of Jesus Christ. Christ demands that He
be the top priority in our lives or we cannot be His followers.
6. God demands that a person coming to Him must first repent or turn
away from all his sins and surrender to Jesus Christ as Lord.

It is our hope that you, having read this far, are interested enough to
continue to examine this message in more detail. What is your soul
worth to you? Jesus said, "For what is a man profited if he gains the
whole world, and loses or forfeits himself?" (Luke 9:25).

WHAT IS GOD LIKE?
God is our Almighty, Sovereign Creator

God is revealed to us in the Bible as the Almighty, Sovereign Creator of the universe and everything in it, including man. "For by Him (God) all things were created, both in the heavens and on earth, visible and invisible...all things were created by Him and for Him" (Colossians 1:16)

Since God is our Creator, we are responsible to Him; both to follow Him and to obey Him. We have no rights of our own. "Know that the Lord Himself is God; it is He who has made us, and not we ourselves; we are His people and the sheep of His pasture" (Psalm 100:3).

As our Creator, it is God who sets the standards of what is right and what is wrong. We have lovingly been created in God's own image. We are not like the animals; nor are we robots or machines. Because He is our Creator, God has an absolute claim on our lives; we are responsible to Him, and totally dependent upon Him.

God is Holy, Righteous, and Just

God is a holy God. He is absolutely pure and of perfect moral excellence. God is worshipped by heavenly beings for His holiness. Seraphs (created beings similar to angels) surround God's throne and cry out, "Holy, holy, holy is the Lord of hosts" (Isaiah 6:3). No other characteristic of God is repeated three times like this in all the Bible. God's holiness is reflected in the purity of His moral law. "So then, the law is holy, and the commandment holy and righteous and good" (Romans 7:12). Because God is holy, He hates all sin and everything which is contrary to His laws.

God is also righteous and just. This means He always does what is right and acts with complete justice in everything He does. Divine justice requires that punishment must be rendered to all rebellion against God's authority and all violations of His moral law. When people commit crimes on earth, we expect them to be punished. Much more should we expect a holy God to punish those who rebel against Him and violate the laws of heaven.

Because He is Holy, Righteous, and Just,
God is a God of Great Wrath

Wrath is one of the characteristics of God which most people prefer to ignore or even try to explain away. In reality, there are more references in the Bible to God's wrath than to His love. "God's wrath is the holiness of God stirred into activity against sin."[1] Sin is any act of or form of rebellion against God's authority or God's laws. "For the wrath of God is revealed from heaven against all ungodliness and unrighteousness of men" (Romans 1:18).

Hell is real. Hell is a place of everlasting punishment and eternal fire. To tell you anything different or try to cover up or ignore the reality of hell would be to lie to you. All people in this life who continue to reject God's authority over their lives and violate His laws will spend eternity in hell. Since sin brings such great punishment, it is very important that we learn more about sin.

SIN AND THE TOTAL CORRUPTION OF MAN'S HEART

"God made man upright; but they have sought out many devices" (Ecclesiastes 7:29).

Few will deny the reality of sin, but most do not view sin as their own personal problem. Where did sin come from? How did the world get into the condition we find it today? The answers to these questions can be found only in the Bible. We have seen that God created man in His own image. The first man, Adam, was created holy and righteous by God. Adam was more than just the first man. It pleased God to make Adam the federal representative or legal head of the entire human family which would be born after him. He was the federal head of the race and all mankind would stand or fall with him. He was therefore given a test to determine whether or not he would obey and serve his Creator and be subject to His authority. "And the Lord God commanded the man, saying, 'From any tree of the garden you may eat freely; but from the tree of the knowledge of good and evil, you shall not eat, for in the day that you eat from it you shall surely die'" (Genesis 2:16-17). Adam voluntarily and willfully chose to disobey God and the entire human race became legally guilty in him. "Therefore, just as through one man sin entered into the world, and death through sin, so death spread to all men, because all sinned" (Romans 5:12). Death (the penalty for sin) came to all men, because all legally sinned in Adam, the federal head of the race. Adam's sin was imputed or charged to all his descendants.

Adam's sin carried with it many severe consequences. Man's very nature or heart became totally corrupted as a result of his sin. Every child who comes into this world is born with a corrupt heart. "The wicked are estranged from the womb; these who speak lies go astray from birth" (Psalm 58:3). A child does not have to be taught to sin or do wrong. One of the first words out of every baby's mouth is "No!" spoken in defiance of authority. The greatest problem man has is his corrupt heart. "The heart is more deceitful than all else, and is desperately sick"(Jeremiah 17:9). Man's corrupt heart causes him to want his own way and to be hostile toward God, His authority, and His laws. Natural man loves himself and hates God so that "those who are in the flesh cannot please God" (Romans 8:8).

Man's corrupt heart is demonstrated by:

1) Selfish Thoughts and Actions. The selfishness within us all demonstrates that our hearts are corrupt. Selfishness is operating my life on the principle that I will do whatever is best for me. If I am faced with two choices, I will choose the one which helps me or benefits me the most. The Bible says, "All of us like sheep have gone astray; each of us has turned to his own way" (Isaiah 53:6). That is the essence of sin: going our own way or doing our own thing and at the same time ignoring God. But the Bible clearly teaches that this is sin because in going my own way, I have made myself king of my life instead of God. I have denied God His rightful place as Ruler and Lord of my life and exalted myself as the god of my own life. That is a terrible evil. Such a tendency in all men demonstrates the total corruption of the human heart.

2) Disobedience to God's Laws. Having become legally guilty in Adam, we then compound that guilt by willingly and knowingly choosing to break God's laws. When we break God's laws we are guilty of fighting God. One of the best places to look to more fully understand God's laws is the Ten Commandments in Exodus 20:1-17. Let's look closely at several of them.

"You shall have no other gods before me" (Exodus 20:3). What are some things people worship instead of God? Many people today worship money, material possessions, popularity, clothes, fame, power, pleasure, or even themselves. People devote their hearts to other things and these things become objects of worship to them.

"You shall not steal. You shall not bear false witness against your neighbor. You shall not murder. You shall not commit adultery" (Exodus 20:15-16 & 13-14). Stealing, lying, murder, and adultery are all forbidden by God. God considers all stealing to be sin. God considers every lie to be sin, even lies we consider to be "white lies."

God's law regulates not only outward actions, but inner thoughts as well. Jesus explained in His Sermon on the Mount that God considers anger of the heart to be equivalent to murder and lustful thoughts to be equal to adultery. How do you feel about the demands made by God's laws? When you compare your own life to God's laws, what is your reaction? In your opinion, what should God do to those who break His laws? James tells us, "For whoever keeps the whole law, and yet stumbles in one point, he has become guilty of all" (James 2:10). Just one violation of the law of God, either in thought or action, makes a person guilty of breaking all of God's laws. We are guilty in Adam's original sin. We are guilty of selfishly exalting and honoring ourselves above God. We compound our guilt by breaking God's laws every day of our lives. Our hearts are totally corrupted by sin. Our sin is indeed very great.

GOD'S SOLUTION:
THE PERSON OF JESUS CHRIST

Prophet
Deuteronomy 18:18

Priest
Hebrews 7:17 & 21-22

King
Revelation 19:16

God's solution to man's problem of a corrupt heart is found in the Person of Jesus Christ. Because God is holy, righteous, and just, only perfect obedience to His laws could qualify a man for heaven. Man's sinful heart renders him incapable of perfect obedience to God's laws.

In the Person of Jesus Christ, God literally became a man and lived a perfect life of righteousness in obedience to His own laws on behalf of His children. Having perfectly obeyed the law, Christ then willingly died for sinners. Divine justice must be satisfied. Sin against God's laws brings death as a punishment. "For the wages of sin is death" (Romans 6:23). When Jesus died, He endured the wrath, anger, and punishment of God for sins. Christ died as a sacrifice for sins, satisfying the requirements of divine justice, and took upon Himself the punishment due for sins. After dying for sinners, three days later Christ arose from the dead. After appearing to His followers over a period of forty days, He ascended into heaven where He now reigns as King and Lord of all creation.

Jesus Christ - Mediator Between God and Men

"For there is one God, and one mediator also between God and men, the man Christ Jesus" (I Timothy 2:5). Jesus Christ is the only mediator between God and men. If men have any hope at all to be saved from their sins, that hope is found only in the Person of Jesus Christ. As mediator, Christ has three offices: Prophet, Priest, and King.

As **Prophet,** Christ teaches us to see into our own hearts. The one taught by Christ as Prophet sees the awful corruption and evil inside of his heart, the worthlessness of what the world offers when compared to heavenly riches, and our need to be taught by Him to follow Him in obedience to all His commands.

As **Priest,** Christ fulfilled all righteousness by perfectly obeying the law of God. As the Old Testament priests offered up their sacrifices to God on behalf of men, so Jesus Christ became the perfect and final sacrifice, dying as a man for men. In so dying, He took the punishment and penalty for the sins of men that God might justly offer to save those from their sins who come to the Lord Jesus Christ for forgiveness and reconciliation to God. "But now once at the consummation of the ages He has been manifested to put away sin by the sacrifice of Himself" (Hebrews 9:26).

As **King,** our wills must be surrendered to Christ so that we submit to His government and rule over us being willing to obey His commandments. Many desire the benefits of Christ's death and forgiveness, but are not willing to submit to His rule over them. They want Christ and their sins, too. But those who will not have Christ as Lord over all their lives cannot use Him as Savior. Those who refuse Christ as their King will one day face Him as their Judge. Christ must be received in all of His offices as Prophet, Priest, and King, freely, willingly, and lovingly by all who would come to Him. You cannot divide the Person of Christ.

COUNTING THE COST

Christ often warned the crowds that listened to Him of the high cost of becoming His follower. On more than one occasion, Jesus chased away potential followers because He knew they were not willing to make the level of commitment which He demanded (John 6:60-66 & Luke 9:57-62). It is very important that anyone who is considering becoming a follower of Jesus Christ first sit down and count the cost of doing so. Christ, in warning of the cost of following Him, said, "For which one of you, when he wants to build a tower, does not first sit down and calculate the cost, to see if he has enough to complete it?" (Luke 14:28). J.I. Packer has written: "In common honesty, we must not conceal the fact that free forgiveness in one sense will cost everything."[2]

Let's look at what Jesus Christ demands of those who are considering following Him. "He who loves father or mother more than Me is not worthy of Me; and he who loves son or daughter more than Me is not worthy of Me" (Matthew 10:37). Here Christ says that our love for Him must be much greater than our love for any others, even our own families. No human relationship should in any way hinder our following Christ, even if that means breaking off that relationship. "And he who does not take his cross, and follow after me, is not worthy of me" (Matthew 10:38). In Jesus' day, a cross was an instrument of torture and death. The one who loves his own life more than Jesus is not worthy of being his follower. Christ is saying that devotion to Him must be greater than love for self, even to the point of giving our lives for Him.

"So therefore, no one of you can be My disciple who does not give up all his own possessions" (Luke 14:33). Jesus Christ must take priority over anything and everything we own. If we love things or possessions more than God, we cannot be followers of Jesus Christ. Jesus demands to be first priority in our lives. Christ must be a higher priority than family; a higher priority than self; a higher priority than possessions or we cannot be His followers.

Count and Compare

You should also consider another important factor. The benefits in coming to Christ far outweigh the sacrifice of giving up all to follow Him. Bishop J.C. Ryle in his book Holiness listed several things which should always be considered in counting the cost of true Christianity. They are summarized here:

1) Count the profit and the loss. You may lose some of the things of the world, but you will gain the salvation of your soul.

2) Count and compare the praise and the blame. You may receive the scorn and blame of blind, sinful men, but you will receive the praise of God.

3) Count and compare the temporary pleasures of sin and the happiness of serving God. The pleasures the world offers are shallow, temporary, and do not satisfy. The happiness and joy which come from following Christ will never leave you, even in death. That joy is lasting and not dependent upon health and circumstances.

4) Count and compare the troubles that Christianity may bring with the troubles the wicked will receive for all eternity in hell. Living a life of self-denial to the glory of God is not easy, but it is nothing compared to experiencing the wrath of God for all eternity. A single day in hell will be far worse than anyone here on earth could ever imagine.[3]

THE RESPONSE GOD CALLS FOR:
REPENTANCE AND FAITH

In speaking to the crowd on Mars Hill, the Apostle Paul declared about God, "God is now declaring to men that all everywhere should repent" (Acts 17:30). The Lord Jesus Christ also spoke of the necessity of repentance saying, "Unless you repent, you will all likewise perish" (Luke 13:3). Since Christ declared that if a person did not repent, they would perish, it is essential that we understand what repentance is.

What is Repentance?

Repentance is the personal recognition of the wickedness and inner corruption of one's heart. This inner corruption has resulted in every man willfully rebelling against God's authority over his life and voluntarily breaking His laws. The truly repentant person sees his sin and even his life as evil and wicked before a holy God and desires to abandon completely his life of sin and turn whole-heartedly to God, desiring to live in obedience to Him. "Let the wicked forsake his way, and the unrighteous man his thoughts; and let him return to the Lord" (Isaiah 55:7).

Repentance demands a forsaking of all known sin and an abandoning of a life of self-pleasing with a full intent to live a life of obedience and service to God from that day forward. Paul wrote the Thessalonians: "You turned to God from idols to serve a living and true God" (I Thessalonians 1:9).

Repentance is not simply a fear of judgement. Repentance is not cleaning up your life by forsaking just a few of your sins. The repentant sinner hates all sin (especially his own) including those sins he formerly loved, and turns his back on them, turning completely to God, to love and serve Him forever. Repentance demands a radical change in behavior.

What is Genuine Faith?

The faith about which the New Testament speaks and demands from every man is faith in a Person. That Person is the Lord Jesus Christ; however, faith is much more than just believing a few facts about Jesus and His death for sinners. Only a person who sees his desperate need will come to Christ in genuine faith. A person convicted of his sins agrees with God that God would be just in sending him to hell for all eternity and that in himself he is spiritually bankrupt and has no hope.

A person expressing saving faith sees Jesus Christ as his only hope. He sees Christ's righteous life as his only hope of fulfilling God's law. He sees Christ's death for sinners as his only hope of receiving forgiveness for his sins. He sees submission to Christ's rule over him as his only hope of being freed from his lusts, the desire to run his own life, the pull of the world, and the bondage of sin.

Genuine faith involves the surrender of the whole life to Jesus as Lord and submitting to His authority over your life. The word "Lord" means ruler or master. A master is someone who has authority over us. When we surrender to Jesus as Lord, we are denying our right to rule over our own lives anymore and willingly submitting to the authority of Jesus Christ. "That if you confess with your mouth Jesus as Lord, and believe in your heart that God raised him from the dead, you shall be saved" (Romans 10:9).

Genuine faith also involves a willingness to obey. The Lord Jesus said, "My sheep hear my voice, and I know them, and they follow Me; and I give eternal life to them" (John 10:27-28). Following Christ is the natural result of believing in Him. Speaking about The Lord Jesus, the writer to the Hebrews said, "He became to all those who obey Him the source of eternal salvation" (Hebrews 5:9). You cannot separate faith and obedience. We do not mean to suggest that the believer lives a life of sinless perfection. Those who believe in Christ do commit sin, but the desire of the true believer's heart and the direction of his life is one of obedience to God. A true Christian hates sin and desires to please God through an obedient life.

Having considered what has been said thus far, it becomes very important for you to consider in your own heart the following questions...

ARE YOU WILLING TO TURN AWAY FROM ALL YOUR SINS AND WILLFULLY PURSUE A LIFE OF RIGHTEOUSNESS INSTEAD?

ARE YOU WILLING TO GIVE UP THE RIGHT TO RUN YOUR OWN LIFE AND SUBMIT TO THE AUTHORITY OF JESUS CHRIST?

ARE YOU WILLING TO BE OBEDIENT TO JESUS CHRIST IN ALL AREAS OF YOUR LIFE AND BECOME HIS FOLLOWER FOREVER?

DIRECTIONS TO THE UNCONVERTED

As you meditate on these questions, search your own heart using the instructions written here:

1) Don't be deceived by a false peace. If you know in your heart that Christ is not the first priority in your life, is not the Lord of your life, then resolve in your heart to seek God until you find Him.

2) Meditate on your sins. Ask God to show you how He views your sin. Until a man is thoroughly sick of sin and hates his own sin, he cannot come to Christ. Think about the number of your sins. Think about your past sins committed through years of rebellion against God. Meditate on the sins of your thought life, the sins of your words, and the sins of your deeds. Think about the punishment your sins deserve. Realize that if you die with your sins unforgiven, the infinite wrath of a holy God will punish you for them for all eternity. Ask God to bring conviction of sin to your heart and help you to hate all sin, even the sins you are most in love with.

3) Realize that there is nothing you can do to save yourself. Without God's work in your heart, you cannot be saved. As long as you rely on your own power and ability to help yourself out of your condition or just "make a decision" to follow God, you will fall short. Your only hope is in God, that He will have mercy on you. Jesus said, "The things impossible with men are possible with God" (Luke 18:27). Therefore, beg for the help of the Holy Spirit and in prayer ask Him to enable you to repent and turn away from all your sins. Ask God to help make your heart willing to surrender everything you have to Jesus Christ and make Him supreme Lord of all your life. Ask Him to change your heart and beg Him to have mercy on you.

Also, do not neglect the means which God has provided to enlighten you. At every opportunity go hear the preaching of God's Word. Read the Bible and meditate upon what it says. As you seek God the following Scriptures may be helpful to meditate on:
Romans 3:10-18, Psalm 51:1-17, Luke 18:9-14, Isaiah 53:3-12 (these verses speak of Jesus Christ), and Luke 5:12-13.

Keep on asking for and seeking God's mercy until you are certain He has answered. Do not be fooled by feelings. Look for real evidence of change in your life. Seek God continually until you find Him. When you are certain He has answered you tell someone you know who is a real Christian and share your joy with him.

---

[1] Arthur W. Pink, *The Attributes of God,* (Grand Rapids: Baker Book House, 1975), p. 83.

[2] J.I. Packer, *Evangelism & the Sovereignty of God,* (Downers Grove, Illinois: InterVarsity Press, 1961), p. 73.

[3] Summarized from J.C. Ryle, *Holiness,* (Welwyn, Hertfordshire, England: Evangelical Press, 1979. First published 1879), pp. 74-75.

4

True Godliness

"But realize this, that in the last days difficult times will come. For men shall be lovers of self, lovers of money...lovers of pleasure rather than lovers of God; holding to a form of godliness, although they have denied its power" (II Timothy 3:1, 2, & 5).

These verses tell us of the condition of men's hearts in the last days. That these men are not saved is evident by the description of them that is given. These verses have much to say to us today, for like these men that Paul was writing about, many today have a form of godliness, but little else. Others do many external works, but may have little more than a form of godliness.

What does it mean to have "a form of godliness?" John Gill said that such an expression refers to those who have an "external show of religion, pretending great piety and holiness, being outwardly righteous before men, having the mask and visor of godliness."[1] These are people who appear to be children of God, who are themselves convinced of their own godliness, but who are, in fact, not Christians at all. Outwardly, they may seem to be among the most religious people we might find in the church, eminent among professors of Christ, but whose hearts have never been changed by God. Charles Bridges in his commentary on Proverbs writes, "We often see this self-deceiver in the spiritual church, exhibiting a full and clean profession to his fellow-men...he has got notions of the grand doctrines of the gospel, and he finds it convenient to profess them. Salvation by free grace is his creed, and he will 'contend earnestly for' its purest simplicity. He conceives himself to distinguish accurately between sound and unscriptural doctrine. He deems it legal(ism) to search for inward evidences, lest they should obscure the glorious freeness of the gospel. All this is a cover for his slumbering delusion. His conscience is sleeping in 'the form of godliness,' while his heart is wholly uninfluenced by 'its power.'"[2]

Statistics: Are They Reliable?

You may be willing to admit that others have been deceived, but what about you? Are you willing to consider that you may be deceived about your standing with Christ? This generation has produced numerous decisions for Christ, but few who are really zealous for the faith. Statistically, Christianity is thriving, but morally America and many other nations are in sharp decline. How can we reconcile such statistics with moral decay and unholy lives among those who profess Christ?

People involved in vacation Bible school, short-term missions projects, evangelistic crusades, revival meetings, and campus ministries typically report on the number of persons who have "accepted Christ" as a result of their ministries. Anyone who questions these statistics is looked on as judgmental or a troubler of Israel. But are these statistics reliable? Is everyone who says they believe in Jesus really a Christian? Ernest Reisinger, author of Today's Evangelism, has said: "This false notion of equating coming forward with coming to Christ has produced the greatest record of false statistics that has ever been compiled by church or business."[3]

What is the common procedure a soul-winner follows today? Is it not to tell the potential convert several facts they need to know about God, so that they can experience a happy life now and go to heaven when they die? When mental assent is given to these facts, the person is proclaimed to be saved, and instructed by the religious worker, church member, or pastor never again to doubt his salvation. But, is this the religion of Jesus? Is Christianity really that easy? Jesus talked repeatedly about "denying yourself" and "taking up the cross"; He said that the way was "hard" and that "few find it."

Evangelical Christianity in its zeal to win souls for God has reduced the gospel message to "just believe." It is commonly taught that any man may be saved at any time if he will just "make a decision" or "accept Christ." Let me ask you a question. Do you believe that if a person admits he is a sinner, believes that Jesus died for his sins, and accepts Jesus as his personal Savior that they will be saved? If your answer is "yes" then you are believing something less than what the Bible teaches; something that is a product of modern religious tradition. Jesus is far more than just a Savior. He is the risen, exalted Lord of the universe and unless you are willing to submit to Him as Lord, all the belief in the world will do you no good. Simply believing yourself to be a sinner is of no merit before God either. Judas, Pharaoh, and Ahab all acknowledged their sins and they all went to hell. The gospel of Jesus Christ is far different than giving mental assent to a few facts or making a decision. Is it possible that many of those who have made decisions, including yourself, have been deceived about what Christianity is all about? Is false conversion spoken of in the Bible? Did Jesus warn us about these things?

Is False Conversion Taught in the Bible?

Numerous Scriptures tell us that many "believe" but are not saved. Jesus frequently warned of those who were outwardly religious, but who would not inherit the kingdom of God in such passages as the parables of the sower (Luke 8:4-18), the wheat and the chaff (Matthew 13:36-43), the wise and the foolish builders (Luke 6:46-49), and the ten virgins (Matthew 25:1-13). Puritan Anthony Burgess wrote regard-ing the parable of the ten virgins, "By this parable it should seem, that a professor having no more than a false, imperfect, or counterfeit work of grace, may live and die with a great deal of comfort and confidence, as if his condition were exceeding(ly) good, and not find it otherwise till it be too late."[4]

Paul spoke of those who had "believed in vain" (I Corinthians 15:2), warned the Galatians of his fear that he had labored over them in vain (Galatians 4:11), and wrote Titus about those who "profess to know God, but by their deeds they deny Him" (Titus 1:16). The writer to the Hebrews speaks of those blessed with spiritual privileges above many in the church today, but who later apostatized or fell away from the faith (Hebrews 6:4-6). These Scriptures speak loudly to us that many who say they are Christians may, in fact, not be Christians at all. A person who walks an aisle or repeats a prescribed prayer (even though that person may feel he prays it sincerely) is not necessarily saved. Something more than believing facts about Jesus and making a profession of faith is necessary for salvation. An outward profession of faith in Jesus Christ is not a reliable indicator of whether a person truly had been saved by God or not. Yet in most churches today, that is the only criterion by which profession is evaluated. A person may do all a counsellor, religious worker, or television evangelist tells him to do and yet still be lost, spend eternity in hell, and yet have no indication of it until he dies, and then it is too late. False conversion is not only Biblical, it is extremely common in our day.

RIGHT ACTIONS,
WRONG MOTIVATIONS

But, how could a person be sincere in his own mind, in praying a prayer for salvation or in doing religious works which he thinks are pleasing to God and still go to hell? Can there be any difference between similar actions performed by different men? The answers to these questions lie in the motivation of the heart of the person. The question is not so much one of what you are doing, but why are you doing it? What deep within your heart is the real reason you are doing it? What's your motive? Why? "All the ways of a man are clean in his own sight, but the Lord weighs the motives" (Proverbs 16:2).

John tells us in his gospel of rulers who believed in Jesus in John 12:42-43: "Nevertheless many even of the rulers believed in Him, but beause of the Pharisees they were not confessing Him, lest they should be put out of the synagogue; for they loved the approval of men rather than the approval of God." It says clearly here that these rulers believed in Jesus Christ, but their belief was merely intellectual, since their actions were designed to meet the approval of men rather than the approval of God. They were men pleasers, preferring the honor and respect of men of high rank rather than the praise of God. Jesus asks the penetrating question of others of like mind, "How can you believe, when you receive glory from one another, and do not seek the glory that is from the one and only God?" (John 5:44). Here the Lord Jesus states plainly that genuine belief is impossible when a person values men more than God. Heart motivation is critical. Unless the heart has been changed, so that a man loves God more than anyone or anything else (Matthew 22:36-38), whatever faith or belief he has will be found defective and only bring a more severe judgment.

The Righteousness of the Pharisees

The Pharisees were a religious sect existent at the time of Christ who had a reputation for being godly and zealous in their religious practice. That the Pharisees were held in high esteem is evident since Christ used them as a standard of righteousness in the Sermon on the Mount (Matthew 5:20). Who were more righteous than they? They prayed, fasted, were zealous in religious duties, memorized the Scriptures, eagerly sought new converts, and were outwardly obedient to the Law. Yet the Lord reserved His sharpest denunciations for them, because although obedient outwardly in many areas, inwardly their hearts were rotten and their motives corrupt.

What was the motivation behind the religious zealousness of the Pharisees? "But they do all their deeds to be noticed by men...they love the place of honor at banquets, and the chief seats in the synagogues, and respectful greetings in the market places, and being called by men, Rabbi (teacher)" (Matthew 23:5-7). The Pharisees used religion to serve themselves and their own selfish desires. Their religion was only a vehicle for self-exaltation and getting what they wanted out of God. They used God to achieve their own purposes. Did it show on the outside? No. Even Christ acknowledges, "you outwardly appear righteous to men" (Matthew 23:28). An ordinary onlooker could not tell that the Pharisees were inwardly corrupt and headed for hell.

All this can help us draw some conclusions: 1) A person may believe in Jesus Christ, but be lost and go to hell. 2) A person may appear to live in conformity to the Law of God, be outwardly obedient, and yet not be serving God, but serving themselves instead. 3) A person whose inner motivation is to honor himself cannot savingly believe the gospel.

A. W. Pink lists three characteristics of the religion of the Pharisees: First, their righteousness "was an external one only, consisting of certain outward observances of the law. Second, their observance of God's law was a partial one: they laid far more stress upon its ceremonial precepts than upon its moral requirements...Third, their actions proceeded from unsound principles: self-interest, rather than the glory of God, was their ruling motive."[5] It is the last of the three we shall examine next.

THE RELIGION OF SELF

The religion of the Pharisees was not that much different than the religion of many professing Christians today. All their religious activities were done to be noticed by men, so that men might praise them and that their own reputations might be enhanced, to use God for their own selfish purposes, in order to please themselves. But the Bible tells us that when we live to please ourselves, we cannot please or serve God. Jesus said, "No man can serve two masters" (Matthew 6:24). Self-sufficiency, an independent spirit, selfishness, and having your own way are all characteristics of those who are in the kingdom of Satan, not the kingdom of God.

There are many things on the surface of Christianity which appeal to self and selfish interests. Jonathan Edwards, one of the greatest American theologians, wrote in the 18th century: "Thus sometimes, under common illuminations, men are raised with the ideas of the natural good that is in heaven; as its outward glory, its ease, its honor and advancement, a (realization of their) being there the objects of the high favor of God, and the great respect of men and angels, etc. So there are many things exhibited in the gospel, concerning God and Christ, and the way of salvation, that have a natural good in them, which suits the natural principle of self-love...That kind of affection to God or Jesus Christ, which does thus properly arise from self-love, cannot be a truly gracious and spiritual love; as appears from what has been said already: for self-love is a principle entirely natural, and as much in the hearts of devils as angels; and therefore surely nothing that is the mere result of it, can be supernatural and divine...selfish, proud man naturally calls that lovely that greatly contributes to his interest, and gratifies his ambition."[6]

It is interesting to note that another characteristic of those whom Paul describes as "holding to a form of godlines,", is that they "shall be lovers of self" (II Timothy 3:2). James tells us that selfish ambition does not come from God, but is demonic and that where selfish ambition exists there is "disorder and every evil thing" (James 3:14-16). William Webster has written: "there are basically two master dispositions in existence in this world. There is the mind of Christ which is the mind of a servant and is charcterized by selflessness; and there is the mind of Satan which is characterized by selfishness. One is controlled by the will of God and oriented towards God's interests; the other is controlled by self-will and oriented towards self's interests. Self-will is Satanic in nature. It is the antithesis of the nature of Christ."[7]

The Scriptures plainly teach that selfishness, going our own way is one of the primary roots of sin. "All of us like sheep have gone astray, each of us has turned to his own way" (Isaiah 53:6). "And the dogs are greedy, they are not satisfied. And they are shepherds who have no understanding; they have all turned to their own way" (Isaiah 56:11). "Behold you have spoken and have done evil things, and you have had your way" (Jeremiah 3:5). "For they all seek after their own interests, not those of Christ Jesus" (Philippians 2:21). Nor did Christ seek to do His own will while on the earth, as He stated many times, "For I have come down from heaven, not to do My own will, but the will of Him who sent Me" (John 6:38).

It is essential for each one of us to ask himself, "What fundamentally controls my life? Who am I living for? Is it self or is it God?" Do you live to please yourself or do you live to glorify God? You cannot do both. Do you care more about what others think of you than what God thinks of you? The one who lives to please himself, in reality, makes himself his own god.

What about your love for God? Do you love God because of who He is: for His holiness and purity, for His righteousness and justice; or do you love God for what He can do for you, for the benefits gained by following Him? Is the underlying principle in your love for God really one of selfishness and self-love? If you live to please yourself in this life, you will die eternally. Is this not what Jesus meant when He proclaimed, "Whoever wishes to save his life, shall lose it" (Mark 8:35)?

The religion of many professing Christians today is based on nothing more than their own self-interests: what helps them, benefits them, contributes to their own well-being. Such is not the religion of Jesus Christ. What about you? Is this your religion? Are you living for self or for God?

WHAT CONSTITUTES TRUE GODLINESS?

True godliness must be founded upon an accurate understanding of God, ourselves, Jesus Christ, and the demands Christ makes of those who would follow Him. But it consists of more than just a right understanding, it consists of a right heart from which right actions proceed. We have seen that external obedience to God means nothing if it does not come from right motivations and right principles. A willing submission of the heart and life to the words and ways of Jesus Christ and a surrender to His authority are essential to true Christianity. Let's look at each of these areas separately.

A Right Understanding About God

A right understanding about God is foundational to our knowing Him. But God must be viewed differently by the one who is apart from Him than by the one who is His child, because the basis of their individual relationships to God proceed from two different foundations. The one who is a child of God views God as a loving Father, but the one apart from God has no right to claim God as his Father by redemption, since he has not been redeemed. Just as a human child views their own father differently than a stranger that they do not know; the unsaved person does not know God, is alienated from Him, and cannot claim the rights and privileges of one who is in His family.

Consider the possiblity that even though you are very religious, that you may be lost. One who is in that position has no right to claim any of the mercies of God relative to salvation. Jonathan Edwards wrote: "God is under no manner of obligation to show mercy to any natural man, whose heart is not turned to God."[8] You must then see God not primarily as the bestower of benefits and mercies upon you, but as your judge. From this perspective there are several aspects of God's character it would be well for us to consider: God is 1) the Sovereign Creator, 2) Holy Lawgiver, and 3) Righteous Judge of the universe and all that is in it.

The sovereignty of God can best be defined as the exercise of His supremacy as King of kings and Lord of lords over all His creation. "Divine sovereignty means that God is God in fact, as well as in name, that He is on the Throne of the universe, directing all things, working all things 'after the counsel of His own will' (Ephesians 1:11) ...unrivaled in majesty, unlimited in power, unaffected by anything outside Himself."[9]

As Sovereign Lord of all, God created all things in the universe, including man, and all men are responsible to submit to His authority; to follow, serve, and obey Him. We have no rights of our own. Natural man desires sovereignty over God, he has no desire to surrender his will to the will of another; but God as Creator has sovereignty over His creature man, and may demand of him whatever He pleases.

Above all else God is a holy God. "God is light and in Him there is no darkness at all" (I John 1:5). He is absolutely pure and of perfect moral excellence. God's holiness is reflected in the purity of His moral law. God's moral law, as revealed in the Ten Commandments, defines sin and calls men to absolute obedience, not just external, but internal obedience, in thought as well as deed.

God has not only given us His law, one day He will judge all men by their response to that law. God is a righteous judge who will punish all sin, every act of disobedience. Those who live as they please and expect to fool God, act as if they believe God is a fool. Any single offense against an infinite, holy God demands infinite punishment. "He that does not obey the Son shall not see life, but the wrath of God abides on him" (John 3:36). God will punish eternally all who reject His authority over them as Lord by sending them to hell, the lake of fire.

A Right Understanding of Ourselves

All natural men are born as rebels against this holy God whom they hate. This rebellion may be traced back to Adam's act of disobedience to God in the garden of Eden when he responded to the tempting words of the serpent to Eve, "You will be like God" (Genesis 3:5). All men inherit a ruling principle of sin in their hearts from their rebellious father Adam.

"But far from owning that they hate God, the vast majority of men will not only vehemently deny it, but affirm that they respect and love Him. Yet if their supposed love is analyzed, it is found to cover only their own interests. While a man concludes that God is favorable and lenient with him, he entertains no hard thoughts against Him. So long as he considers God to be prospering him, he carries no grudge against Him. He hates God not as One who confers benefits, but as a Sovereign, Lawgiver, Judge. He will not yield to His government or take His law as the rule of his life."[10] The issue is one of authority and control. Who will be the supreme authority in our lives: the God who created us or self? Man wants to be his own authority. Man wants to run his own life, so he enthrones self as King and Lord of our lives and in doing so, rejects the supremacy and authority of God Almighty. Self is God to us and what we do is dictated by our own selfish desires.

Sin is a principle of hostility and rebellion against God, of independence from God, and the proclamation of man's self-sufficiency as exemplified in living to please self. All the vices of man can be traced to selfishness as their root. What is pride but self-exaltation? What is lust but self-gratification? What is independence but self-rule? What is the attempt to achieve power but a desire to have self-dominion over others? What is lying but a vehicle for self-protection and self-advancement? What is self-sufficiency but the declaration that you have no need of God in your life?

God's law exposes our sin to us when we hear its righteous demands. To pick and choose which commandments we will obey or disobey reveals the heart of a rebel; the heart of one who is acting only for his own self-interests. The Lord God has said, "You shall have no other Gods before me. You shall not bear false witness against your neighbor. You shall not steal. You shall not commit adultery" (Exodus 20:3, 16, 15 & 14). Christ further clarified the meaning of God's law in the Sermon on the Mount by saying that anger in the heart was equal to murder and that lustful thoughts were equal to adultery. James tells us that just one sin, one angry thought, one evil desire makes us guilty of breaking all of God's laws. We are born sinners by nature. We compound our guilt daily by breaking God's laws. Sin possesses us.

A Right Understanding About Jesus Christ

Jesus Christ is the central figure in God's plan of redemption. A wrong understanding about God as revealed in the Person of Jesus Christ is the foundation of false religion everywhere.

In the Person of Jesus Christ, God literally became a man and lived a perfect life of righteousness in obedience to His own laws on behalf of His children. Having perfectly obeyed the law, Christ then willingly died for sinners. Divine justice must be satisfied. Sin against God's laws brings death as a punishment. "For the wages of sin is death" (Romans 6:23). When Jesus Christ died, He endured the wrath, anger, and punishment of God for sins. Christ died as a sacrifice for sins, satisfying the requirements of divine justice, and took upon Himself the punishment due for sins. After dying for sinners, three days later Christ arose from the dead. After appearing to His followers over a period of forty days, He ascended into heaven, where He now reigns as King and

Lord of all creation.

Who is Jesus Christ? He is the risen, exalted Lord of the universe who calls on us to submit to His Word by making it the rule of our lives and offering universal obedience to it through the living of a holy life; to submit to His judgment about us, by owning our sin for what it is, a corrupt ruling principle which dominates every area of our lives and causes us to live only to please ourselves and to undervalue His death by wrongly viewing it as a quick fix to provide forgiveness to us, even if we continue to live in disobedience to Him by living for self; and to submit to His authority by denying ourselves and surrendering to Him as absolute Lord of our lives, being willing to follow Him wherever He may lead, even if it means loss of friends, relatives, estate, possessions, freedom, or life. To follow Him even unto death, if He should so choose. Is this the Lord you follow? Many desire the benefits of Christ's death and forgiveness of sins, but they are not willing to submit to Him as Lord in every area of their lives. You see, it is not enough to simply accept Jesus as your Savior. He is Lord. And those who do not surrender themselves to Him as Lord cannot use Him as a Savior. Only by submission to Christ as Lord can one receive forgiveness of sins.

THE DENIAL OF SELF & THE GLORY OF GOD

What are the demands Christ makes of those who would follow Him? Jesus repeatedly issued calls to those who expressed interest in becoming His followers to deny themselves using such words as, "If anyone wishes to come after Me, let him deny himself, and take up his cross, and follow Me" (Matthew 16:24; see also Mark 8:34-38, Luke 9:23-25, Matthew 10:37-39, and Luke 14:25-33).

We have seen that the essence of sin is selfishness or living for self. When Christ calls on men to deny themselves, He is striking at the very heart of sin in our souls. There is no greater tension in the gospel message than the call to self-denial. If a man from one country were to go to the neighboring country and yank the crown off the head of the King of that country, do you think there would be an uproar? Likewise when the King and God of Self is attacked, what a great uproar there is in the soul of natural man who desires to cling to his corruption and maintain the Godhead of Self.

So what does it mean to deny self? Self-denial involves renouncing the supremacy and rule of self as Master over our lives. It is a forsaking of all things for Christ: the forsaking of hidden lusts and sins, the forsaking of the world and all it offers, the forsaking of living for myself to please myself. It is a forsaking of all idols, whatever they may be, so that nothing is loved more than Christ. Writing about self-denial in the 17th century Thomas Hooker said: "It is a harder thing than you are aware of; you must deny life and all, and not only some profits and pleasures in life; yes and have it not only in a readiness to be bound, but to die for the Lord Jesus or to suffer anything for Him. Oh it is not an easy thing to deny a man's self...can you deny life, liberty, lands, livings? Is it easy to go to prison? You that have secret lusts, is it easy to leave them? Oh know that it is not easy to be a Christian."[11]

But this self-denial must have a proper object. Christ tells us in Mark 8:35: "Whoever loses his life for My sake and the gospel's shall save it." Please note what the Lord says, "For My sake." At the heart of self-denial is the giving up or forsaking of your own will, for the will, interests, and priorities of another, the Lord Jesus Christ. When self is denied, Christ becomes the chief object of love, trust, faith, and dependence. Christ becomes Master in place of self. Christ spoke of plucking out right eyes and cutting off right hands to illustrate the radical nature of the gospel duty of self-denial or repentance. For Biblical self-denial as described here is the essence of repentance. Turning from sin and self to God in Christ, living now for Jesus' sake, with the ultimate purpose in life being the same as His: to glorify God.

The man-centered theology of today would have us believe that God exists primarily for the benefit of man. Such is not the case. God did not create the world or man primarily so that He could bless man, but so that *He* might be glorified. The glory of God is the supreme end of God's creation of both the world and man. The Word of God tells us plainly that men are to seek God's glory as the chief end of all they do: "Whether, then, you eat or drink or whatever you do, do all to the glory of God" (I Corinthians 10:31).

Thus, failure to live for the glory of God is sin. Whatever man does, if it is not for the glory of God, it is sin. Since none of the actions of natural man are done to glorify God, everything he does is sin. "The plowing of the wicked is sin" (Proverbs 21:4, KJV). When the natural man eats, he is sinning. When he works, he is sinning, because his primary motive in doing it is only to benefit himself and not to glorify God.

Other Scriptures testify clearly that man exists to bring glory to God. "Let your light shine before men in such a way that they may see your good works, and glorify your Father who is in heaven" (Matthew 5:16). "Not to us, O Lord, not to us, but to Thy name give glory" (Psalm 115:1). "Whoever speaks, let him speak, as it were, the utterances of God; whoever serves, let him do so as by the strength which God supplies; so that in all things God may be glorified through Christ Jesus, to whom belongs the glory and dominion forever and ever" (I Peter 4:11). Puritan Richard Baxter writes of the real reason men do not seek after God's glory, saying, "Pride causeth men to set up their supposed worth and goodness above or against the Lord; so that they make themselves their principal end, and practise that which some of late presume to teach, that it is not God that can or ought to be man's end, but himself alone: as if we were made only for ourselves, and not for our Creator. Pride makes men...value God, but as they do their food, or health, or pleasure, even as a means to their own felicity (happiness); not as preferring Him before themselves, nor making Him the chiefest in their end. They love themselves much better than God."[12]

In denying ourselves for the glory of God man becomes what he was meant to be, a servant of the living God. This was the nature of Jesus Christ when He was on the earth; He "emptied Himself, taking the form of a bond-servant" (Philippians 2:7). Christ calls on men to deny themselves, take up their cross, and follow Him, to live "for His sake" and not for their own. If we live for ourselves we violate the supreme end of our creation: to live for the glory of God. He who will not deny Himself for Christ's sake cannot be His disciple. He who will not give up all he has when called to do so is not a follower of Christ. He who loves anything more than Christ is not a Christian. You cannot follow Christ on cheaper, easier terms than these. Christ requires a complete surrender of the heart, will, and life to Him. Nothing less than this will suffice.

THE GOSPEL OF HISTORIC CHRISTIANITY

Most who profess Christianity today show little interest in or knowledge of what those who have gone before us taught or believed. They have possibly heard the names of people such as John Bunyan or Jonathan Edwards, but they know very little about their theology. This is tragic. It is wise to consider how the Holy Spirit has led godly men in past times in church history to see how our current teaching compares with theirs. Let us examine the beliefs of some men of the past regarding self, self-denial, and commitment to Christ.

Thomas Hooker was one of the first Puritan leaders in New England. In 1640 he authored a book entitled *The Christian's Two Chief Lessons* in which he wrote the following regarding the natural man: "As men do expect all from themselves, so they aim at themselves in whatever they do; they make their own persons the end of their actions; they do homage to self and sin, and look not to the obeying of God; so everything is wrought for a man's self...thus a natural man is nothing but self; so it is in every particular. Because men naturally being blind, do conceive their own credit and excellence to be the chiefest good; and this is the main cause we make our selves our gods...so a man sets up self above all, and it will be a god... you would have grace, and you would be saved, but you will not have it on Christ's terms, you will not deny your selves, which must be, if ever you be saved by Christ."[13]

John Bunyan is perhaps best known today as the author of *Pilgrim's Progress,* the largest selling book in history, next to the Bible. In a work entitled *Come and Welcome to Jesus Christ* Bunyan stated: "Coming to Christ is attended with an honest and sincere forsaking all for him. "If any man come unto Me, and hateth not his father and mother, and wife and children, and brothers and sisters, yea, and his own life also, he cannot be My disciple; and whosoever doth not bear his cross and come after Me cannot be My disciple" (Luke 14:26-27). By these and the like expressions elsewhere Christ describeth the true comer, or the man that indeed is coming to him; he is one that casteth all behind his back; he leaveth all, he forsaketh all, he hateth all things that would stand in his way to hinder his coming to Jesus Christ."[14]

David Clarkson was an associate of the great John Owen and later followed him as pastor of Owen's church upon his death. Clarkson wrote an entire treatise on Luke 14:27 from which the following words are taken: "He that is not content, when he is called to it, to be separated from nearest friends and dearest relations, to part with his country and habitation, to be stripped of his estate and outward accommodations, to be deprived of his liberty, and whatever else is dear to him in this world, he is not for Christ's turn, He cares for no such followers...For He that is a Christian indeed, he loves Christ above all, but he that will not part with relations, estate, country, liberty, for Christ's sake, he loves them better than he loves Christ: for that a man loves most which he will least part with. He that will not part with them all, rather than sin against Christ, has not the love of a disciple for Christ, and so is not indeed a Christian."[15]

Jonathan Edwards is perhaps the best known and greatest of America's theologians. In 1746 he authored a book which is still regarded as a classic work, *Religious Affections.* In it Edwards describes what belongs to a true profession of Christ: "The Holy Scriptures do abundantly place sincerity and soundness in religion, in making a full choice of God as our only Lord and portion, forsaking all for him, and a full determination of the will for God and Christ, on counting the cost; in our hearts closing and complying with the religion of Jesus Christ, with all that belongs to it, embracing with all its difficulties, as it were hating our dearest earthly enjoyments, and even our own lives, for

Christ; giving up ourselves, with all that we have, wholly and forever, unto Christ, without keeping back anything or making any reserve; or in one word, in the great duty of self-denial for Christ; or in denying, i.e. as it were disowning and renouncing ourselves for him, making ourselves nothing that he may be all."[16]

Numerous other references could be given from equally respected men. Let these suffice to demonstrate that what has been said so far is amply supported by some of the greatest Christian leaders in history.

NEW HEART, NEW LIFE

Of what else does true religion consist? The Lord Jesus, speaking about the scribes and Pharisees, quoted Isaiah the prophet, saying, "This people honors Me with their lips, but their heart is far from Me. But in vain do they worship, teaching as their doctrines, the precepts of men" (Matthew 15:8-9). These people spoke about God, worshipped God, but all in vain, because their worship came from their lips only, it did not come from their hearts. True religion has everything to do with a heart that is right before God.

Christ told the Pharisees, "You are those who justify yourselves in the sight of men, but God knows your hearts" (Luke 16:15). God knows the hearts of all men and His Word says, "The perverse in heart are an abomination to the Lord. But the blameless in their way are His delight" (Proverbs 11:20). Those who are blameless in their way are contrasted with the perverse in heart because the condition of the heart determines the way of the life.

The heart of the natural man is corrupt and rotten. Almost three thousand years ago the prophet Jeremiah wrote, "The heart is more deceitful than all else and is desperately sick; who can understand it?" (Jeremiah 17:9). This desperately sick, deceitful heart must be changed by the supernatural power of God if a man is ever to become one of God's true children. Only with a change of heart will any man submit to Christ's demands to deny himself and surrender to Him as Lord.

The Scriptures tell us of the radical change in heart and nature that accompanies salvation. The Apostle Paul described it this way, "If any man is in Christ, he is a new creature, the old things passed away: behold, new things have come" (II Corinthians 5:17). The writer to the Hebrews tells us that without holiness no one will see the Lord (Hebrews 12:14). A holy, godly life is the result of a change in heart. When the heart is changed a man's motivations change, his values change, his reasons for living change, his attitude toward sin changes. He now loves God above all else, he longs to read God's Word that he may know Him better, he desires to be obedient to all of God's commandments.

Obedience to God's commandments, both externally and internally, proceeding from godly motivations is a sure sign of a changed life. Jesus said, "He who has My commandments and keeps them, he it is who loves Me" (John 14:21). The Apostle John wrote: "And by this we know that we have come to know Him, if we keep His commandments. The one who says, 'I have come to know Him,' and does not keep His commandments, is a liar, and the truth is not in him" (I John 2:3-4). Without this change of heart accompanied by a corresponding change of life, no man can rightfully call himself a Christian.

Don't be deceived by a false peace. External religious activity and peace in the heart are no guarantee of genuine conversion. Multitudes are in hell right now who were sure that their souls were secure. There is a false peace which comes from the devil and not God. If you know upon examining your life that you are living for self instead of the glory of God, that Jesus is not the Lord of your life, then commit yourself to seeking God now until you find Him.

The Sovereignty of God & The Use of Means

Should you desire to seek God in truth, the first thing you must understand is that only God can change your heart and save you. Your hope is not to be found in walking an aisle, repeating the words of a prescribed prayer, or making a decision. None of these will change your heart. Your only hope is in God, that he will have mercy on you. For God has said, "I will have mercy on whom I have mercy" (Romans 9:15). Hope is not to be found within yourself, in something you do, or in your own wish to become a Christian. It is not any more in your power to change your heart than it is for you to create a world. "So then it does not depend on the man who wills or the man who runs, but on God who has mercy" (Romans 9:16). You are locked up on death row and you have no key to release yourself. Unless God chooses to have mercy on you, you will be lost forever.

All sinners deserve immediate damnation. It is in God's power to execute that sentence now, to defer it until a later date, or to wholly and completely save you from it because of His mercy in and through the death of Christ. God may choose to have mercy on you, He may not. He is free to do as He pleases. But the one who does not seek, certainly will not find. The one who is too lazy to pursue God with all his heart will fall short of the goal.

You must face the sinfulness of your own life and heart. Until you are willing to expose the corruption of your heart to the searching light of the Word of God, you will never forsake your sins. Ask God to help you hate your sin, even the sins you are most in love with. Meditate on your sins, the sins of your thought life that no one but you and God know about, the sins of selfishness which have dominated your lifestyle, and the sins of past actions. Think about the punishment your sins deserve. Ask God to convict you deeply of all your sins. Until a man is thoroughly sick of sin, he will not come to Christ.

Beg for the help of the Holy Spirit and in prayer ask Him to enable you to repent and turn away from all your sins. Ask God to help make your heart willing to surrender everything you have to Jesus Christ and make Him the supreme Lord of all your life. Pray that God would grant unto you the gift of faith. Ask Him to change your heart and beg Him to have mercy on you.

Also, do not neglect the means which God has provided to enlighten you. At every opportunity go and hear the faithful preaching of God's Word. Read the Bible and meditate upon what it says. As you seek God the following Scriptures may be helpful to meditate on:
Romans 3:10-18, Psalm 51:1-17, Luke 18:9-14, Isaiah 53:3-12 (these verses speak of Jesus Christ), and Luke 5:12-13.

Keep on asking for and seeking God's mercy until you are certain He has answered. Do not be fooled by feelings. Look for real evidence of change in your life. Seek God continually until you find Him. When you are certain He has answered you tell someone you know who is a real Christian and share your joy with him.

[1] John Gill, *Exposition of the Old & New Testaments, Volume 9,* (Paris, Arkansas: The Baptist Standard Bearer, Inc., 1989), p. 333.

[2] Charles Bridges, *Proverbs,* (Edinburgh: Banner of Truth, 1988), p. 601-602.

[3] Ernest Reisinger, Sermon delivered to the Southern Baptist Founders Conference, July 1987.

[4] Anthony Burgess, *Spiritual Refining,* (Ames, Iowa: International Outreach, Inc., 1990), p. 3.

[5] Arthur W. Pink, *An Exposition of the Sermon on the Mount,* (Grand Rapids: Baker Book House, 1982), p. 62.

[6] Jonathan Edwards, *Religious Affections,* (Binghamton, New York: Yale University Press, 1959), p. 277, 242, & 246.

[7] William Webster, *The Christian,* (Edinburgh: Banner of Truth, 1990), p. 28.

[8] Jonathan Edwards, *The Works of Jonathan Edwards, Volume 1,* (London: Ball, Arnold, and Co., 1840), p. 352.

[9] Arthur W. Pink, *The Attributes of God,* (Grand Rapids: Baker Book House, 1975), p. 32.

[10] Arthur W. Pink, *Gleanings From the Scriptures,* (Chicago: Moody Press, 1969), p. 114.

[11] Thomas Hooker, *The Christian's Two Chief Lessons,* (London: T. B., 1640), p. 49.

[12] Richard Baxter, *Baxter's Practical Works, Volume 1,* (Ligonier, Pennsylvania: Soli Deo Gloria, 1990), pp. 195-196.

[13] Thomas Hooker, *The Christian's Two Chief Lessons,* (London: T. B., 1640), pp. 40-41 & 51.

[14] John Bunyan, *Bunyan's Complete Works,* (Philadelphia: Bradley, Garretson & Co., 1871), p. 570.

[15] David Clarkson, *The Works of David Clarkson,* Volume 1, (Edinburgh: Banner of Truth, 1988), p. 450.

[16] Jonathan Edwards, *Religious Affections,* (Binghamton, New York: Yale University Press, 1959), p. 397.

5

Are You Deceived?

"The hypocrite's hope shall perish" (Job 8:13).

Even though we have spoken of man's corruption and of what true godliness consists, I fear there are many who read these lines who are still deceived about their own condition before God. Most men have a confident persuasion that their hearts are good when they are not. In order to unmask even further the hypocrisy of the human heart we must probe deeper, for "man's heart is a matchless cheat, and self-delusion (is) so reigning and so fatal a disease, that I do not know which is greater, the difficulty or the necessity of the undeceiving work that I am now upon. Alas for the unconverted, they must be undeceived, or they will be undone! But how shall this be effected?"[1]

Throughout the Scripture we see pictures being painted of the unconverted. Their heart attitudes are revealed to us in many places in God's Word. The heart of a natural, unconverted man will gravitate toward the things he loves the most, whether it be the world, power, sensual pleasure, money, notoriety, gluttony, or whatever. Natural man's projects and plans are all directed toward himself as his ultimate end. How men express their lusts may be vastly different from one man to the next. The purpose of this chapter is to expose the evil of sin and how it is manifested in the lives of men. We shall examine the specific sins of three types of unconverted men: the profane man, the moral man, and the unconverted religious man. In order to see sin for what it is in the lives of those who practice it, let us look at these men individually. It is granted that not all men will fit into one catagory exclusively. A religious man may be much like the moral man in many respects. A moral man may have the characteristics of both the religious and the profane. The sons of Eli were priests and yet were openly profane. Any general portrait will be subject to variation where applied specifically to individuals, but these portraits will help us to see sin more clearly. I urge you for the sake of your eternal soul, do not read over these lines quickly, but study them and apply them to your heart and conscience. Philip Doddridge wrote: "The physicians of souls must speak plainly, or they may murder those whom they should cure."[2] Speaking sweet, melodious sounds which do not pierce the heart may please your ears, but they will not benefit your eternal soul. So I will speak plainly, with the hope and prayer that many who read these lines will be undeceived and led to true repentance. We will start with the sin of the profane man.

A PORTRAIT OF THE DECEIVED PROFANE MAN

The profane sinner is an outward breaker of God's holy Law, the Ten Commandments, in both the first table (those commandments dealing with God) and second table (those commandments dealing with man). His philosophy of life is "eat, drink, and be merry for tomorrow we will die." This man is repeatedly spoken of in the Scriptures. He is one who practices deeds which God says are evil, but he is still confident of his own goodness, the integrity of his own heart, and God's acceptance of him. Notwithstanding his own good assessment of himself, he is one who is "foolish, disobedient, deceived, serving divers lusts and pleasures" (Titus 3:3, KJV). He is deceived by the love he has for himself and enslaved by the love of his lusts.

He has no fear of God (Psalm 36:1-2) for he sees God as one much like himself. He pictures God as one all made up of love and One who winks at his lusts. He believes this because God has done nothing to hinder or restrain him in the course of his life. In Psalm 50:21 God rebukes the wicked man for his evil ways and ungodly thoughts about Him, saying: "These things you have done, and I kept silence; you thought I was just like you." Thus he creates a "god" in his own mind to suit his lusts in the hopes that his sins will not be punished. In doing this he dethrones God and sets up an idol in His place.

This profane man is a willful breaker of God's laws and seeks either to stretch or make void God's commandments. If he lies, he believes he has good reason to do so. If he curses or uses foul language, it is only so that he will be accepted by others like himself. If he commits adultery or fornication, it is only to satisfy his "God-given desires." If he drinks too much and becomes drunk, it is only in good fun and to forget the burdens of life: after all he thinks, Jesus turned water into wine at the wedding feast in Cana, didn't He? His attitude toward God is "God has forgotten; He has hidden His face; He will never see it. What does God know? Can He judge through the thick darkness?" (Psalm 10:11 & Job 22:13). The Lord speaks about such men in Jeremiah 9:2-3 & 5: "For all of them are adulterers, an assembly of treacherous men. And they bend their tongue like their bow; lies and not truth prevail in the land; for they proceed from evil to evil, and they do not know Me...they have taught their tongue to speak lies; they weary themselves committing iniquity."

The profane sinner prefers that you keep your religion to yourself and not trouble him with your beliefs, for such things are personal and private matters. "Keep quiet. For the name of the Lord is not to be mentioned" (Amos 6:10). He tells himself that all is well with his soul (Luke 12:19), for he believes in God and his heart is good, even though his actions are evil. He compares himself to others and magnifies their faults so that he might seem better in his own eyes. While deep inside his real feeling toward God is "What is the Almighty, that we should serve Him? And what profit should we have if we pray to Him? Therefore they say unto God, 'Depart from us; for we desire not the knowledge of Thy ways'" (Job 21:15 & 14, KJV).

This man is typified in Scripture by the lives of Esau, the man's man, who sold his own birthright for a bowl of stew; Ahab, the covetous and deceitful king; and the prodigal son prior to his conversion to God, who wasted his substance on riotous living. This man may approve of himself, but God sees him differently. The damning error of the profane man is that he does not believe that breaking God's laws will matter, because he does not think that God really cares that much about sin. His sin consists in the rejection of God's laws and God's authority over him, to rule and command him. God is not fooled by his vane excuses for living the way he does. God says plainly to the profane sinner: "Do you not know that the unrighteous shall not inherit the kingdom of God? Do not be deceived: neither fornicators, nor idolators, nor adulterers, nor effeminate, nor homosexuals, nor thieves, nor the covetous, nor drunkards, nor revilers, nor swindlers, shall inherit the kingdom of God" (I Corinthians 6:9-10). "All liars shall have their part in the lake which burns with fire and brimstone" (Revelation 21:8, NKJV). Do any one of these lifestyles describe you? Are you an adulterer? Are you covetous? Are you a drunkard? Are you a liar? If so, the mark of the damned is upon you and without sound repentance you will be lost forever. "For the ways of a man are before the eyes of the Lord, and He watches all his paths. His own iniquities will capture the wicked, and he will be held with the cords of his sin" (Proverbs 5:21-22). Profane man, do not lie to yourself. You are not fooling God. You are only deceiving yourself.

A PORTRAIT OF THE DECEIVED CIVIL OR MORAL MAN

The deceived civil or moral man is one who outwardly practices some of the duties of the second table of God's Law which pertain to conduct towards men, while neglecting those duties of the first table which pertain to God and the worship of God. Thomas Hooker describes this man as "one as is outwardly just, temperate, chaste, careful to follow his worldly business, will not hurt so much as his neighbor's dog, pays every man his own, and lives of his own; no drunkard, adulterer, or quarreler; loves to live peaceably, and quietly among his neighbors."[3] He might be likened to the rich young man in the gospels to whom Christ said, "Keep the commandments." The rich young man responded, "All these things have I kept" (Matthew 19:17 & 20).

The civil or moral sinner's life is characterized, from his own perspective, by good intentions and good dealings with men. He hopes to do as well as the best of men in what he does. His trust lies in himself. His reformation comes from within himself and the good he does is of his own making. He brings his base appetites under control and sees moral perfection as consisting in his conformity to his natural conscience. He is a self-made man. He does not understand that the Word of God condemns him repeatedly: "Cursed is the man who trusts in mankind, and makes flesh his strength, and whose heart turns away from the Lord" (Jeremiah 17:5) "In Thy sight shall no living man is righteous" (Psalm 143:2). Samuel Crook wrote: "The Moralist looking back neither to Adam, nor forward to Christ, seeth neither the evil of the disease, nor the comfort of the remedy; and so knoweth neither himself, nor God."[4]

This moral man considers that by doing his duty to man, he is thus discharged from doing his duty to God. He is civil so he thinks that he does not need to be religious. What need does he have of church, prayer, or reading the Bible? He is honest and sincere toward men, keeps his word, pays his taxes, and does all that the most respectable citizen does. He believes that God thinks of him in the same way as he sees himself: "I am innocent, surely His anger is turned away from me" (Jeremiah 2:35).

He measures his righteousness by his own corrupt judgment without the aid of God's word and therefore, he is able to excuse many sins which he commits toward God and man because of his good intentions. He does not realize that God is not impressed with his deeds. The Lord has sworn to punish men who proclaim their innocence: "Behold, I will enter into judgment with you because you say, 'I have not sinned'" (Jeremiah 2:35). "It is an evil thing and bitter, that thou hast forsaken the Lord thy God, and that My fear is not in thee, saith the Lord God of hosts" (Jeremiah 2:19, KJV). "There is not a righteous man on earth who continually does good and who never sins" (Ecclesiates 7:20). "There is a way that seems right to a man, but its end is the way of death" (Proverbs 16:25).

The civil or moral man's goodness can be attributed to several things: education, government, the company he keeps, and/or the example of others. His goodness cannot be ascribed to himself, but to those who raised him, the government whose laws he obeys, the morality of those he keeps company with, and the example of those whose respect he desires. In reality, the moralist loves man and not God. He is a man-pleaser. Much of what he does is done to gain the respect, admiration, and applause of others, so that *he* might be esteemed. Again God's Word rebukes him: "Stop regarding man, whose breath of life is in his nostrils; for why should he be esteemed?" (Isaiah 2:22).

Although he strives to keep the outside of his walk upright before men, inside the moral man is filled with spiritual corruptions. He sees no evil in pride or self-pleasing, but esteems both of them as virtues. He exalts self-love; in fact, he nourishes and cherishes it. He performs virtuous actions so that other men might love him and that he might love himself more. All his actions proceed from self and self-love. But the things that he considers virtues, God considers vices. God hates his pride and selfishness because they exalt self in the place of God. "Every one that is proud in heart is an abomination to the Lord" (Proverbs 16:5). Moral man, do you realize that your pride stinks in the eyes of God? "I will punish the world for their evil, and the wicked for their iniquity; and I will cause the arrogancy of the proud to cease" (Isaiah 13:11). In the 17th century Richard Baxter wrote: "Wickedness is an inclination and addictedness to devotedness to ourselves above God, or as separated from God; and this inclination, disposition, or separation of man to himself instead of God, is it that I call self or selfishness...The principal part of it consisteth in an inordinate self-love. This is a corruption so deep in the heart of man, that it may be called his very natural inclination, which therefore lies at the bottom, below all his actual sins whatsoever; and must be changed into a new nature, which principally consists in the love of God. This is original sin itself, even the heart of it. This speaks what man by nature is; even an inordinate self-lover; and as he is, so he will act. In this, all other vice in the world is virtually contained."[5] The self-love that the moral man thrives on is at the heart of nearly every sin that men commit.

This man also greatly errs in his understanding of how God's law will be applied in the judgment of sinners. He considers nothing evil which is hidden from the eyes of man, but God does not judge by outward appearance. The civil man in order to judge of himself rightly must look at God's holy law as applied to the inward thoughts of a man. Christ plainly tells us that evil thoughts constitute sin just as much as evil actions. "But I say to you, that everyone who looks on a woman to lust for her has committed adultery with her already in his heart" (Matthew 5:28). Have you ever looked at a woman and lusted after her? Then, in God's eyes, you deserve to go to hell. "How long will your wicked thoughts lodge within you?" (Jeremiah 4:14). Men will be judged by every thought of their hearts on judgment day, not just by their outward actions.

The moralist errs also in that he compares himself to others who are worse than himself. He is greatly conceited that all will go well for him because so many others are so much worse than he is. He compares himself to the profane man who lives in disobedience to the laws of men and God. Let me ask the moralist: What good does it do to compare yourself to vile men who are clearly on their way to hell? Will that keep you out of hell as well? Still he thinks, 'I do no harm to others and many think well of me,' but it is not a negative righteousness (consisting in not harming others) which God seeks in men. The fruit tree in the orchard that does not bear good fruit is cut down, not because it does no harm to other trees, but because it does not produce that which the grower desires. "Every tree that does not bear good fruit is cut down and thrown into the fire" (Matthew 3:10). Still the moralist will argue that he is more righteous than many who profess religion and who believe they will go to heaven. This appears *to him* to be a powerful argument that his estate is good, but he does not consider that many who profess religion are themselves lost and headed for hell. He does not distinguish between an outward professor of religion and the one who truly possesses eternal life. He is ignorant of Christ's words to those seeking salvation: "Strive to enter by the narrow door; for many, I tell you, will seek to enter and will not be able" (Luke 13:24).

In reality, the civil or moral sinner is no different than the religious hypocrite whom he condemns. The religious hypocrite outwardly pays God the worship that He commands while committing sins and neglecting the doing of good to men. The moral man prides himself that he has done his duty to man (however imperfectly), but he miserably fails in doing his duty to God. God requires men to worship Him in spirit and in truth: that men pray, read His word, hear His word proclaimed, and sanctify His sabbaths. The moral man never complies with these duties to God, but condemns the religious hypocrite for neglecting his duties to men. Daniel Dyke wrote of the hypocrisy of the moral man: "*Unhonest religion is as good as irreligious honesty*. And if in thy judgment the former be naught, surely the latter cannot be good. Religion, or the fear of God, Solomon calls the head of all goodness: Honesty then without religion is as a body without a head, even a rotten and stinking carrion, and wilt thou yet be so fond as to think it is a sweet smelling sacrifice in God's nostrils?"[6]

Most wicked of all, the moral man is unwilling to bow his knees or heart to Jesus Christ as Lord. He sees no need of Christ for he, by his good intentions and good works, has become the savior of himself. While he thinks of himself as neutral to Christ, Christ sees him as an enemy: "He who is not with Me is against Me; and he who does not gather with Me scatters" (Matthew 12:30). Those who have no need of the blood of Christ in this life, shall pay eternally for their sins in the next life. The Scriptures plainly declare: "By the works of the Law no flesh will be justified in His sight" (Romans 3:20).

The civil or moral man is typified in Scripture by the rich young man who came to Christ asking, "What shall I do to obtain eternal life?" (Luke 18:18). Although the moral man does not spend much time considering eternity, he feels he has done all to comply with any terms that there might be to obtain eternal happiness for himself. The damning error of the civil or moral man is that he does not, *internally* in his heart and mind, keep the commandments of God and he fails to perform those duties of worship to God which God requires. He is ruled by the deceitfulness of selfishness and self-love. Jesus Christ speaks to the moral man: "For from within, out of the heart of men, proceed the evil thoughts, fornications, thefts, murders, adulteries, deeds of coveting and wickedness, as well as deceit, sensuality, envy, slander, pride, and foolishness: All these evil things proceed from within and defile the man" (Mark 7:21-23).

A PORTRAIT OF THE DECEIVED RELIGIOUS MAN

The deceived religious man is one who is an outward practicer of the duties of the first table of the Law, dealing with the worship of God, but whose inner motivations for his religious worship are grounded in himself and the advancement of himself, not the glory of God. He is a frequenter of public worship assemblies, a hearer of the word of God, and a receiver of the ordinances of baptism and of the Lord's Supper. He may have a great deal of knowledge of the word of God as did the lawyer who spoke to Christ (Luke 10:25-29). He may pray a great deal as the Pharisee in Christ's parable did (Luke 18:9). He may fast as King Ahab (I Kings 21:27) and the hypocrites in Isaiah's time fasted (Isaiah 58:3). He may have very high regard for the preachers of God's word as Saul did for Samuel and even entertain them in his own home (Luke 14:1); and yet, for all his external religion, he is deceived in his own heart and unless he repents he will die and go to hell. "For circumcision, baptism, hearing, receiving, and all such like badges of outward profession, they are but as the outward garment of Christians, which may be easily put on by those that are none."[7] If the devil cannot draw men away to worship idols then he seeks to keep men self-satisfied in external service and exercises of worship, while all the time they believe in their hearts that this is all God requires of men.

The religious sinner is punctual in his external duties of religion. He is precise in the things which can be observed by those in the world, but takes liberty with the rest. He is like those who came to hear the prophet Ezekiel who "speak to one another, every one to his brother, saying, 'Come, I pray you, and hear what is the word that cometh forth from the Lord.' And they come unto thee as the people cometh, and they sit before thee as my people, and they hear the words, but they will not do them: for with their mouth they show much love, but their heart goeth after their covetousness" (Ezekiel 33:30-32, KJV). They *hear* the words of God, but *they do not do them.* This religious man is careful to attend church, to pray, to read his Bible, but his obedience to the commands of God is a limited and partial obedience. He picks and chooses what he will abide by and what he will not abide by. "A hypocrite's† obedience is always a limited and stinted obedience. It is either limited to such commands which are most suitable to his ease, safety, honor, profit, pleasure, etc., or else it is limited to the outward part of the command, and never extends to the inward and spiritual part of the command."[8] He is like the harlot in Proverbs 7:14-15 who told the young fool she had come to seduce: "I was due to offer peace offerings; today I have paid my vows. Therefore I have come out to meet you, to seek your presence earnestly, and I have found you." Like the harlot, the excellency of his external religious practices allows him to be lenient with himself regarding his own sins. He is like the religious man spoken of by Solomon in Ecclesiastes 5:1: he offers the sacrifice of fools and yet he does not know that he is doing evil.

The religious man uses religion to achieve his own ends and purposes. It soothes his conscience. It covers him with a cloak of respectibility. His good deeds bring him the praise and applause of men. It

---

† It is important to understand that a man may be a hypocrite and not realize it. "Some deceive both themselves and others, and think they are no hypocrites, but are as confident of their honesty and sincerity, as if they were no dissemblers at all: but yet they are as verily hypocrites as the former, because they seem to be religious and sincere, when indeed they are not, though they think they are; and profess themselves to be true Christians, when they are nothing." Richard Baxter, Works, Volume 1, p. 176.

may bring him greater material profits and enrich him. Puritan Thomas Brooks wrote that pleasure, profits, and honor are the primary ends the hypocrite lives for in this world: "They are his trinity which he adores and serves, and sacrifices himself to. Hypocrite's ends are corrupt and selfish...A hypocrite is all for his own glory; he acts for himself, and from himself. So that I may have the profit, the credit, the glory, the applause, come of God's glory what will."[9] "Nay, doubtless, in the very duties of religion, in praying, hearing, reading, and the like, they are but serving self, while they take on them to serve God; and their holiest devotions are but such a serving of God, as flatterers will serve their prince or landlord with, merely that he may do them a good turn, and may serve their ends, and be serviceable to them."[10] God is near to their lips, but far from their minds (Jeremiah 12:2). "The haters of the Lord would pretend submission to Him" (Psalm 81:15).

This man's religion is borrowed from others. He is like the Pharisees and Sadducees who went out to hear John the Baptist, whom John warned, "Do not suppose that you can say to yourselves, 'We have Abraham for our father.' (Matthew 3:9). This man is frequently in the company of zealous Christians and believes that his association with them somehow accounts to his credit. "He hath a good father, so had Manasseh; or a good friend, so had Ahithophel; or a good master, as Gehazi. Of these he speaks much in good company, that he may seem to be somebody himself...that by the names he useth, he may gain reputation of savouring of the same spirit."[11] That many good Christians and even ministers speak well of him strengthens him in his belief that his profession is sound, as if a pat on the back by a godly man is enough to guarantee him entrance into heaven. But it is vain to trust in the good opinions of others! Thomas Watson wrote: "Alas, one may be gold and pearl in the eye of others, yet God may judge him reprobate silver; others may think him a saint, and God may write him down in His black book. Judas was looked upon by the rest of the apostles as a true believer."[12] Those duties he does do are performed either from custom, habit, or education like those in Isaiah's time of whom the Lord said, "This people draw near Me with their mouth, and with their lips do honour Me, but have removed their heart far from me, and their fear toward Me is taught by the precept of men" (Isaiah 29:13).

The man who is religious, but lost, applies the promises of the gospel to himself, but not the threatenings. He is content to hear ministers preach on the love and mercy of God, but he does not like to hear of the difficult and more demanding teaching of the Scriptures (Luke 14:26-33). The less spoken about sin and holiness, the more he is at ease. He considers preaching on obedience to be legalistic and beneath the grace of the gospel. He longs to hear about free forgiveness, unlimited grace, and the eternal happiness of the redeemed. He is like those of old who said to the prophets, "You must not prophesy to us what is right, speak to us pleasant words, prophesy illusions" (Isaiah 30:10). He is a man of much talk, but little or no fruit. He is an inhabiter of castles in the sky and builder of houses upon sand. But Christ warned such men, "The one who has heard, and has not acted accordingly, is like a man who built a house upon the ground without any foundation; and the torrent burst against it and immediately it collapsed, and the ruin of that house was great" (Luke 6:49).

The religious man talks much of his own experience and of religion, but in daily life he thinks little about God or heaven in comparison to the things of the world. Spiritually, he is a sluggard when it comes to private duties of religion. He spends little time wrestling with God in prayer, little time thinking of the lost, for his mind is set principally on the world and the things of the world. He may have a thousand thoughts about the world and worldly things in comparison to one thought about God, but still he assures himself that his soul is secure. His covetousness is hidden under such labels as providing for his family or earning more so that he can give more to the Lord's work. "What are all the thoughts of unsanctified men employed for, but for themselves and theirs?...The thoughts of one man runs upon his covetousness, and another man's upon his filthy lusts, and another man's upon nothing but selfish things...morning and evening, at home or abroad, as the thoughts of the sanctified are on God, and heaven, and the way thereto, so the thoughts of the unsanctified are all upon self, and the interest of self, and the means thereto."[13] Christ rebukes the religious man who is covetous saying, "Beware, and be on your guard against every form of greed; for not even when one has an abundance does his life consist of his possessions" (Luke 12:15). "You cannot serve God and mammon (money)" (Matthew 6:24).

This religious man thinks he is a follower of Christ, but in reality he has no experimental knowledge of the truth. His great error lies in the assumption that he believes, while, in reality, his faith is in his own faith. He thinks he trusts God with much, but really he leans upon himself. He strengthens his good opinion of himself with reasonings such as this: "I believe, because I profess the same with others that do believe."[14] He may trust God as one trusts someone with a small package or something that is out of date, but not with anything important to him. This is seen in his response to sufferings or when temporal dangers and trials assault him. In such troubles, which concern only the outward man, his faith fails him. He believes in God as long as God is good to him, but if trouble arises, so do his doubts and anxieties. Daniel Dyke wrote of such men, "These men, that so confidently profess that they believe that God hath provided super-abundant riches of glory hereafter for them, cannot believe that He will provide competent necessaries of maintenance for this present life, whence they tremble in dangers."[15] God's word says, "You believe that there is one God. You do well; the demons also believe, and shudder" (James 2:19). The devils believe and fear and tremble. This man believes a lie and presumes about himself. His faith is a fancy: a trusting in himself and his decision. O religious sinner, you are like those in Sardis: "you have a name that you are alive, but you are dead" (Revelation 3:1).

The religious man desires the blessings offered by Christ, but not Christ as He is offered in the Scriptures. He is willing to share with Christ in eternal happiness and heaven, but not willing that his life should be changed and made holy on earth. He is willing to be forgiven and redeemed by Christ, but he is not willing to submit to the laws and government of Christ. He is willing for Christ to give him temporal blessings (prosperity, health, happiness, etc.) and to receive glory from Him, but not willing for Christ to command him and rule over him. He says with the hypocrites, "This man shall not rule over us" (Luke 19:27). He embraces a Christ of his own creation who exists only in his own imagination. His real desire is for earthly blessings, not spiritual ones. He is willing to receive blessings in heaven when he dies (for heaven is certainly far better than hell), but he will not part with his treasure on earth (Mark 10:21-22). He comes to God to get from God, not to give up all that he has for Him (Matthew 13:46). He has Christ because he thinks he has Him and not even the words of Christ Himself will wake him up.

Although the actions of the religious sinner may be good in them-selves, his inner motivations for doing the things that he does are wrong (pride, self-seeking, desire for gain, etc.) and this ruins and destroys all. God weighs the heart and searches the motives of men in all that they do (Proverbs 16:2). Outward actions do nothing to win favor with God if the motives behind those actions are wrong. God seeks that men would glorify Him in all that they do. What are the motives inducing the religious hypocrite to service? "Self-ends are the operative ingre-dients in all a hypocrite does; self is the chief engine, self is the great wheel that sets all a hypocrite's wheels going. When hypocrites take up religion, it is only to serve their own turns, to bring about their own carnal ends; they serve not the Lord, but their own bellies...No man can go higher than his principles, and therefore a hypocrite having no higher principles than himself, all he does must needs be terminated in himself...A hypocrite always makes himself the end of all his service."[16] Thomas Hooker wrote: "An appearing outward agreement is not that which may give hope that our profession is sound, but we must have an eye to the integrity of the heart in the performance thereof."[17] The religious Jews in the time of the prophet Malachi offered sacrifices to God, but God was not pleased with them because their motives were wrong: "'When you present the blind for sacrifice, is it not evil? And when you present the lame and sick, is it not evil? Why not offer it to your governor? Would he be pleased with you? Or would he receive you kindly?' says the Lord of hosts. 'A son honors his father, and a servant his master. Then if I am a father, where is My honor? And if I am a master, where is My respect?'" (Malachi 1:8 & 6). "The sacrifice of the wicked is an abomination" (Proverbs 21:27). God is not pleased with outward religious duties when the motives of the heart are wrong.

This religious man does not want to be thought by others to be without peace from God, thus he cannot endure to be examined and searched by the Word of God as to the sincerity of his profession. He does not want others to inquire after his personal experience with God. Although he is strongly persuaded that his condition is good, his peace is not from God, but of his own devising. He echoes the words of the foolish, "I shall have peace though I walk on in the stubborness of mine own heart" (Deuteronomy 29:19), but will not join with David in saying, "Search me, O God, and know my heart: try me, and know my thoughts: and see if there be any wicked way in me, and lead me in the way everlasting." (Psalm 139:23-24). He would rather it be supposed that his condition is good because he professes it to be so. The religious man is condemned by the words of Christ: " Therefore take care how you listen; for whoever has, to him shall more be given; and whoever does not have, even what he *seems to have* shall be taken away from him" (Luke 8:18).

Thomas Shepard wrote of such men: "The mind, having been long rooted in this opinion, that I am in a good estate, will not suffer this conceit to be plucked out of it. Now, your old, rooted, yet rotten professors, having grown long in a good conceit of themselves, will not believe that they have been fools all their lifetime, and therefore now must pull down and lay the foundation again...Men grow crooked and aged with good opinions of themselves, and can seldom or never be set straight again. Hence such kind of people, though they would fain be taken for honest, religious Christians, yet will never suspect their estates to be bad themselves, neither can they endure that any other should search or suspect them to be yet rotten at the heart."[18]

The religious man who is lost is typified in Scripture by the Pharisees, who did everything that looked good on the outside, but inwardly were full of dead men's bones; by Demas, who preached the gospel with the Apostle Paul, but forsook Christ, "having loved this present world" more than God; and by Judas Iscariot who was trusted by the apostles with the money bag, but when his dreams of earthly glory faded, betrayed Christ for thirty pieces of silver.

The man who adds a profession of Christ to his own morality is among the most difficult to convince of his unsound profession because he is among the most deceived of all men. Indeed, living for self while at the same time thinking you are following Christ is one of the most common forms of self-deception. Doing good deeds so that men will love you and praise you has pride as its foundation, not Christ. You are only serving yourself. While your life may appear to yourself and others to be acceptable to God, if self is the root of it, it is the very antithesis of Christianity. The damning error of the religious man is that he does what he does in service to God from unsound principles and rotten motives. His inner principles have nothing to do with God's glory and have much to do with his own glory. God speaks to the religious man: "Although you wash yourself with lye and use much soap, the sin of your iniquity is before Me" (Jeremiah 2:22).

A PORTRAIT OF THE HUMAN HEART

Reader, do you see yourself in any of these men? All like these men are headed straight for hell. It does not matter how moral you have been, or how religious you are, or how much better you are than other people. God does not judge the way that men judge. He sees all that you do and knows all of your thoughts and motives: motives which you might even be deceived about due to the blinding power of self-love. "There is a generation that are pure in their own eyes, and yet is not washed from their filthiness" (Proverbs 30:12). Are you one of those that this verse describes? Are you pure in your own eyes, but still polluted with the filth of your sins? Have you ever seen your heart as evil and corrupt before God? Have you ever been broken in spirit before the Lord because of the evil within you? Are you a stranger to prayer, an infrequent reader of the Word of God, a lover of the world? Do you really love Jesus Christ more than all the world and everything in it? What are the true motives behind your religious service?

Perhaps the following illustration quoted by Loraine Boettner from a work by W. D. Smith will help you to see your state before God: "'In a gang of pirates we may find many things that are good in themselves.

Though they are in wicked rebellion against the laws of the government, they have their own laws and regulations, which they obey
strictly. We find among them courage and fidelity, with many other
things that will recommend them as pirates. They may do many things,
too, which the laws of the government require, but they are not done
because the government has so required, but in obedience to their own
regulations. For instance, the government requires honesty and they
may be strictly honest, with one another, in their transactions, and the
division of all their spoil. Yet, as respects the government, and the
general principle, their whole life is one of the most wicked dishonesty.
Now, it is plain, that while they continue in their rebellion they can do
nothing to recommend them to the government as citizens. Their first
step must be to give up their rebellion, acknowledge their allegiance to
the government, and sue for mercy. So all men, in their natural state, are
rebels against God; and though they may do many things which the law
of God requires, and which will recommend them as men, yet nothing
is done with reference to God and His law. Instead, the regulations of
society, respect for public opinion, self-interest, their own character in
the sight of the world, or some other worldly or wicked motive, reigns
supremely; and God, to whom they owe their heart and lives, is
forgotten; or, if thought of at all, His claims are wickedly rejected, His
counsels spurned, and the heart, in obstinate rebellion, refuses
obedience'...The good actions of unregenerate men, Smith continues,
'are not positively sinful in themselves, but sinful from defect. They
lack the principle which alone can make them righteous in the sight of
God. In the case of the pirates it is easy to see that all of their actions
are sins against the government. While they continue pirates, their
sailing, mending, or rigging the vessel, and even their eating and
drinking, are all sins in the eyes of the government, as they are only so
many expedients to enable them to continue their piratical career, and
are parts of their life of rebellion. So with sinners. While the hearts is
wrong, it vitiates everything in the sight of God, even their most
ordinary occupations; for the plain, unequivocal language of God is,
'Even the lamp of the wicked is sin,' (Proverbs 21:4).'"[19] When the
heart is unsound, all the actions which proceed out of it are rotten, even
those which appear good to the eyes of men.

Let us take a closer look at the human heart as God sees it: "Who can
say, I have made my heart clean, I am pure from my sin?" (Proverbs
20:9). Can any one of you say that you have never sinned? "But the
wicked are like the troubled sea, when it cannot rest, whose waters cast
up mire and dirt" (Isaiah 57:20). "Can the Ethiopian change his skin,
or the leopard his spots? Then may ye also do good, that are accustomed

to do evil" (Jeremiah 13:23). Can you change your evil heart by your good intentions or your religious duties? "But we are all as an unclean thing, and all our righteousnesses are as filthy rags" (Isaiah 64:6). Even the supposedly good things you do, that men consider righteous, are rotten and vile before God. "The heart is deceitful above all things, and desperately wicked, who can know it?" (Jeremiah 17:9, KJV).

All men are born defiled with sin. Every day they live they increase and aggravate their guilt before God. The human heart is deceitful above all else. Men love themselves and refuse to judge themselves according to God's laws, always seeking to lessen or ignore their guilt. They would be clean when they are filthy. They would be pure when they are vile. They would be saved when they are lost. All such deception ends at death, but then it is too late. How long will you continue to live in deceit? The profane sinner deceives himself by not believing that God hates all sin and will punish it just as He has promised. The moral sinner deceives himself by not believing that the thoughts of the heart and mind are just as important to God as outward actions. The religious sinner deceives himself by his lack of under-standing that inner motives are critical to God, not just outward forms of worship. How long will you live in self-deception? How long will you continue cherishing a good opinion of yourself, when God is filled with anger toward you for your wickedness?

Your wicked heart is the source of all the sins you commit. Jesus Christ said: "For from within, out of the heart of men, proceed the evil thoughts, fornications, thefts, murders, adulteries, deeds of coveting and wickedness, as well as deceit, sensuality, envy, slander, pride, and foolishness: All these evil things proceed from within and defile the man" (Mark 7:21-23). Your sin is your greatest enemy and your great-est problem and you are utterly incapable of doing anything about it outside of Jesus Christ. Jesus Christ is God's only answer to the problem of sin. Only Christ has suffered the penalty for sins by dying on the cross for the sins of men. "Christ was once offered to bear the sins of many" (Hebrews 9:28). "He appeared to put away sin by the sacrifice of Himself" (Hebrews 9:26). Christ came to die for sins that men who are fatally infected with sin might be freed from sin. It is only through complete surrender in faith to Jesus Christ as Lord that a man can be justified before God. "He who believes in the Son has eternal life; but he who does not obey the Son shall not see life, but the wrath of God abides on Him" (John 3:36). The ignoring of Jesus Christ (as profane and moral men do) or giving Him lip service without yielding the heart fully to Him (as the religious man who is lost does) is fatal. Wake up and repent of your life of sin and surrender to Jesus Christ as Lord with your whole heart!

"Do you serve God as if He were a child, or an idol, or a man of straw; that either knoweth not your hearts, or is pleased with toys, and compliments, and shows, and saying over certain words, or acting a part before Him on a stage? Do you know what you offer, and to whom? His power is omnipotency; His glory is ten thousand-fold above that of the sun; His wisdom is infinite; millions of angels adore Him continually; He is thy King and Judge; He abhoreth hypocrites...Doth not the weight of your salvation forbid this trifling? You might better set the town on fire, and make a jest of it, than jest your souls into the fire of hell. Then you will find that hell is no jesting matter. If you mock yourselves out of your salvation, where are you then? If you play with time, and means, and mercy until they are gone, you are undone forever."[20] "Knowest thou not this of old, that the triumphing of the wicked is short, and the joy of the hypocrite but for a moment? Though his excellency mount up to the heavens, and his head reach unto the clouds, yet he shall perish forever like his own dung: they which have seen him shall say, 'Where is he?'" "So are the paths of all that forget God; and the hypocrite's hope shall perish" (Job 20:4-7 & 8:13, KJV).

[1] Joseph Alleine, *An Alarm to the Unconverted,* (Edinburgh: Banner of Truth, 1964), p. 68.

[2] Philip Doddridge, *The Rise and Progress of Religion in the Soul,* (Grand Rapids: Baker Book House, 1977), p. 19.

[3] Thomas Hooker, *The Christian's Two Chief Lessons,* (London: T.B., 1640), p. 213.

[4] Samuel Crook, *Divine Characters,* (London: A.B., 1658), p. 33.

[5] Richard Baxter, *Baxter's Practical Works, Volume 3,* (Ligonier, PA: Soli Deo Gloria, 1990), pp. 394-395.

[6] Daniel Dyke, *The Mystery of Self-Deceiving,* (London: William Stansby, 1633), p. 60.

[7] Ibid, p. 62.

[8] Thomas Brooks, *Touchstone of Sincerity,* (Pensacola, Florida: Mt. Zion Bible Church, nd), p. 6.

[9] Ibid, p. 7.

[10] Richard Baxter, *Baxter's Practical Works, Volume 3,* (Ligonier, PA: Soli Deo Gloria, 1990), p. 400.

[11] Samuel Crook, *Divine Characters,* (London: A.B., 1658), p. 167.

[12] Thomas Watson, *Heaven Taken by Storm,* (Ligonier, PA: Soli Deo Gloria, 1992), p. 32.

[13] Richard Baxter, *Baxter's Practical Works, Volume 3,* (Ligonier, PA: Soli Deo Gloria, 1990), p. 403.

[14] Samuel Crook, *Divine Characters,* (London: A.B., 1658), p. 283.

[15] Daniel Dyke, *The Mystery of Self-Deceiving,* (London: William Stansby, 1633), p. 64.

[16] Thomas Brooks, *Touchstone of Sincerity,* (Pensacola, Florida: Mt. Zion Bible Church, nd), pp. 7-8.

[17] Thomas Hooker, *The Christian's Two Chief Lessons,* (London: T.B., 1640), p. 231.

[18] Thomas Shepard, *The Works of Thomas Shepard, Volume 1,* (Ligonier, PA: Soli Deo Gloria, 1991), p. 73.

[19] Loraine Boettner, *The Reformed Doctrine of Predestination,* (Phillipsburg, NJ: Presbyterian & Reformed Publishing Company, 1932), pp. 69-70.

[20] Richard Baxter, *Baxter's Practical Works, Volume 1,* (Ligonier, PA: Soli Deo Gloria, 1990), pp. 182-183.

6

A Call to Self-Examination

"Test yourselves to see if you are in the faith;
examine yourselves!" (II Corinthians 13:5).

Anthony Burgess has rightly said, "to turn with all the heart to God is a work of great difficulty and rarity...conversion is a rare work."[1] Paul called on the Corinthians to examine their own hearts before God to determine whether they were genuinely saved or not. Even though he had started the church at Corinth, he took nothing for granted when he wrote to them, saying, "Test yourselves to see if you are in the faith; examine yourselves!" (II Corinthians 13:5). What a horrible condition it is for a man to be blessing himself saying: "Soul, take your ease," while at the same time God abhors him. Yet, most men in the world live in this condition.

The great question which a man must resolve in this life is whether he belongs to God or not. "Are you regenerated or are you not?" That is the issue, for Christ has told us through Nicodemus: "Truly, truly, I say to you, unless one is born again, he cannot see the kingdom of God" (John 3:3). Thus, a person's eternal destiny hangs in the balance with the resolution of this issue.

What is regeneration? Regeneration is the divine communication of spiritual life by the Holy Spirit of God to a person who formerly was spiritually dead in trespasses and sins. One older writer described it this way: "It is a work of the Spirit of God, by means of the word of God, infusing holiness into the whole man, for the glory of God, in his salvation...The principal, the sole author is the Spirit of God, the Holy Ghost, the third person of the Trinity. The same Spirit by whom our Saviour Christ's manhood was conceived in His mother's womb, is the sole worker of this conception of grace in the heart."[2]

What then are some of the effects of regeneration in the attitudes and affections of the one who has been regenerated? Through regeneration a man comes to love God as the highest good and the Lord Jesus Christ more than all that the world offers. The one who is regenerated loves the word of God as truth and makes it the rule of his life. His mind, will, and affections are changed. He now hates sin and loves righteousness. His thoughts, aims, motives, and actions are now directed to God's glory rather than to pleasing himself. He loves what he once hated and hates what he once loved. He is quite literally a new creation (II Corinthians 5:17). Through regeneration the heart and life are radically changed by the power of the Holy Spirit. So, are you regenerated, or are you not?

Do not think it is enough for you to answer, "I hope so." Such uncertainty about something so critical is sheer folly. "Let that man that is willing to put off this matter slightly; and to please himself in idle imaginations, saying 'I hope I have been regenerated'; though he have never bestowed pains to inquire into the grounds of this hope; let that man be even almost assured, that he is not as yet regenerated."[3] A sound builder does not fear the examination of his work. Only robbers, thieves, and adulterers shun the light of day. Do not content yourself with such faint hopes of eternity.

Men are often content to live as blind men when it comes to the issue of their souls. They are deceived by their own hearts and think that a strong desire to be happy in the afterlife assures them that it will be so. We desire good for ourselves, therefore we are quickly persuaded to believe we are secure in our current condition. We are deceived by self-love. Self-love causes us to be blind to our sins. When a man believes himself to be as good as most men, and better than many, he naturally concludes, because of the deception of self-love, that God thinks of him in the same way.

Does it do any good for a man to imagine that he is extremely rich when he is really miserably poor? Is it helpful to a man to think that he is in good health when he is dying of a deadly disease? Would it help a man drowning in a lake to suppose himself a great swimmer, when he does not know how to swim? Does it really help you to say you are a child of God, if you are not?

It is far more dangerous to think you are a child of God when you are not, than to fear that you may not be a child of God, when you are. It is better to fear without a sound reason, than to hope without a sound reason. If you are regenerated and you do not know it, it will not be deadly to you; but, if you are not regenerated and you think you are, you are in great danger, because you are headed for hell, in spite of what you think. In hell you will curse yourself for eternity for being such a fool on earth.

William Whately in his 1618 work *The New Birth* listed these among the unregenerate: 1) the ignorant boaster of his own righteousness, 2) a man senseless of his own sinfulness and depravity, 3) the one who gives way to the evil thoughts of his heart and who is not concerned about little sins in his life, 4) the one who clings to a pet sin which he will not part with or repent of, and 5) the profane who are liars,

swearers, drunkards, immoral, covetous, etc. (I Corinthians 6:9-10).
"The unregenerate can never become regenerate, till he first perceive
himself unregenerate. A child of Satan can never be made the child of
God, till he feel(s) himself the child of Satan."[4]

O Lord, strike at the hearts of those who are falsely convinced of their
own goodness and of Your acceptance of them. Let those who are
deceived be undeceived. Let no man who reads these words go away
without intense, soul-searching, self-examination. Cause those clothed
with the deception of self-love to be stripped of that soul-damning love.
Pierce the hearts of sinners who are unregenerate and put within them
a desire to seek you honestly and fervently. Awaken the dead that they
might sense their deadness and the pollution of their hearts and flee to
Christ who alone can save them. Amen.

THE JUSTICE OF GOD IN THE DAMNATION OF MEN

Unregenerate men are filled with sin. Every man is born in this state
and multiplies his own guilt with every day that passes, adding sin to
sin and heaping up judgment upon judgment. "If a man sins against the
Lord, who can intercede for him?" (I Samuel 2:25). "For all have sinned
and come short of the glory of God" (Romans 3:23). "It is appointed for
men to die once and after this comes judgment" (Hebrews 9:27).The
wrath of God presently abides on all who are outside of Christ (John
3:36).

Every sin a man commits is committed against an infinite, holy God
who hates sin and must punish it. No matter how severe or lengthy a
punishment may be, that punishment is just if it is no greater than the
crime. Even the smallest sin committed against an infinite being
demands that infinite punishment be rendered. Thus God is perfectly
just to punish sinners forever for their sins committed on earth.

If you are unregenerate, you stand before God with a heart that is
corrupt and rotten. You have lived all your life as your own authority,
doing whatever you please, when you have been pleased to do it. You
have lived to please yourself and ignored God. You may have given lip
service to God, but it was only that He might be used by you, to fulfill
your selfish desires and bless you. You have never done one thing for
God's glory, but instead, you have strived to bring glory and honor to
yourself.

You have committed sin after sin daily. You have lied since child-
hood to protect your own self-interests. You have had prideful thoughts
and done things primarily that men would look favorably upon you.
You have had covetous thoughts, have envied your neighbor for what

he has, and desired to have it for yourself. You have lived for the things the world offers and paid little or no attention to God. Some of you have had vile and lustful thoughts and have engaged in immoral sexual fantasies, thinking about past sins and dreaming lustfully about future ones.

God has given you life and breath and you have used them to disobey His commandments, living a life of rebellion against your Creator. Your sins cry out to God for Him to exercise His justice and execute His wrath upon you and He would be perfectly just in damning you eternally this very moment. The fact that you have been given another day to live is solely because God has permitted it. "You are in God's hands, and it is uncertain what He will do with you."[5] Should the Lord cast you into hell tonight, He would be righteous and just in doing so, for you deserve it. "But because of your stubbornness and unrepentant heart you are storing up wrath for yourself in the day of wrath and revelation of the righteous judgment of God" (Romans 2:5).

Some of you may have engaged in religious exercises and duties for months or maybe even years. You have prayed often, given money to the church, and been in regular attendance at worship services on Sunday mornings. When you compare yourself with others, you believe you have done more than many have and expect that God should take notice of your prayers and duties. You pride yourself in your religion and in all you have done for God. But if your heart and life have not been changed by the Spirit of God through regeneration, all such religion is worthless. God thinks nothing of what you have done and counts it as less than nothing. It is a stench in his nostrils. "All our righteousnesses are as filthy rags" (Isaiah 64:6, KJV).

Your religion will not commend you to God. Nothing you can do can make up for the sins you have committed. You are utterly lost before a holy, righteous God who has every right to condemn you to hell for all eternity and, until you see yourself in that condition, it is highly doubtful that God will show mercy to you.

Do not suppose that you can obligate God to show mercy to you because of your religious duties. God is under no obligation to show mercy to you and need not do so. You are utterly dependent upon God's sovereign will in all things, even in matters of salvation. God has not obligated Himself to answer wicked men who call upon Him with selfish motives, simply that they may be delivered from His wrath or receive good at His hand. "And they do not cry to Me from their heart when they wail on their beds; for the sake of grain and new wine they assemble themselves, they turn away from Me" (Hosea 7:14).

If all equally deserve God's wrath and God would be just in

condemning them all, then is God not free to choose some from among those deserving hell and damnation and show mercy to them? If He is not free to choose as He pleases, then He must be under obligation to men, and therefore must grant them salvation as a debt owed to them. But God is not a debtor to men. God is under no obligation to any man to save him. God is free to do as He pleases, because He is God. "I will have mercy on whom I have mercy, and I will have compassion on whom I have compassion" (Romans 9:15). God is free to grant salvation to some and to refuse it to others. Your sin makes you a debtor to God, not Him a debtor to you. "Then they will cry out to the Lord, but He will not answer them. Instead, He will hide His face from them at that time, because they have practiced evil deeds" (Micah 3:4). Solomon Stoddard has written: "God has a liberty to bestow His grace upon whom He will. Mercy is God's own, and He will make choice who shall be the subjects of it. God is master of His own gifts, will bestow them on one, and deny them to others. It is just for God to deny sinners saving mercy, but if He pleases to have mercy upon some, none may prescribe who they shall be; but He may choose one, and refuse another."[6] Unless God chooses to have mercy on you, you will be lost forever.

Then again, who knows but what God may be gracious unto you. He has been gracious to others who were as wicked as you and He may do so with you also. There is no lack of sufficiency in Christ to save you. Christ's blood can cleanse the vilest sins. Christ has abundantly suffered for the sins of those whom God has purposed to save. Do not then be discouraged from seeking for mercy simply because you have no guarantee that God will grant you that mercy. It is possible that if you diligently begin to seek God in Christ that you may find Him. The Scriptures encourage you to seek the Lord while He may be found and call upon Him while He is near (Isaiah 55:6). Christ stands and calls to men who are burdened down with their sins, saying, "Come to Me, all who are weary and heavy-laden, and I will give you rest" (Matthew 11:28).

To the end that you may seek God with all your heart, the rest of this booklet has been dedicated to aid you in your search for the mercies of Christ. Apply yourself diligently to all that follows. Make it your life's work to seek the Lord until you find Him. It is the most important task you can pursue in this life. It is worth the laying aside of all other things which might divert you. In order to aid you in your search, I urge you to get a clear sight of your sins and what the Scriptures say about them.

MEDITATION UPON THE SINS OF YOUR HEART AND LIFE

Until sin is clearly seen for what it really is in God's eyes, it is highly unlikely that you will be either convicted deeply by the Spirit of God or convinced to forsake it. It is not simply a recognition or acknowledgment of our sins that pleases God. Many wretched men have been willing to acknowledge themselves sinners and admitted their guilt before God, without being changed in their hearts. Judas, Pharaoh, and Ahab all acknowledged themselves to be sinners. God seeks more than a bare admission of guilt from you. Until your heart is broken over your sins and over the vile and despicable way you have treated God all your life, there is no room for mercy for you.

Labor therefore to get a clear sight of what sin really is. Look into the Scriptures and see the words the Spirit of God has used to describe sin. "The whole head is sick, and the whole heart faint. From the sole of the foot even unto the head there is no soundness in it; but wounds, and bruises, and putrifying sores: they have not been closed, neither bound up, neither mollified with ointment" (Isaiah 1:5-6, KJV). Sin is like a body covered with wounds and putrifying sores oozing with pus. "Their throat is an open grave" (Romans 3:13). Sin is like an open grave revealing a dead body which is decaying and stinks. Peter tells us that sin is like the vomit of a dog and compares it to a pig wallowing in muck and filth (II Peter 2:22). Paul compares it to gangrene which causes the flesh to rot (II Timothy 2:17) and to dung in Philippians 3:8. Thomas Watson has written: "The sinner's heart is like a field spread with dung. Some think sin is an ornament; it is rather an excrement. Sin so besmears a person with filth that God cannot abide the sight of him."[7] And Ezekiel illustrates sin by the picture of a newborn baby wallowing in it's own blood (Ezekiel 16:4-6).

Let us then look at the picture the Scriptures paint of sin: wounds, putrifying sores, the stench of an open grave, the vomit of a dog, a pig smeared with muck and filth, dung, gangrene, and a bloody mess. Sinner can you look at these words and picture their images in your mind? How do you feel when you do so? Are you proud of your sins? Are you at all troubled by your sins? Until a man is thoroughly sick of his own sins and hates them and himself for them, he will not come to Christ rightly. "Then you will remember your evil ways and your deeds that were not good, and you will **loath yourselves** in their own sight for your iniquities and your abominations" (Ezekiel 36:31).

I can hear someone say, "Oh, it pains me to look so clearly and closely at myself." It will pain you far worse to ignore your sins and then be tormented and punished for them in the fires of hell for all eternity! Think about your past sins. You have lived a number of years upon the earth and have you never told a lie? Have you never exalted yourself and sought the attention and admiration of men? Have you never uttered a foul word or used the Lord's name in vain? Have you never sought to be rich or coveted the possessions of another? Have you never had filthy and lustful thoughts? If you are unregenerate, you have lived your entire life to please yourself and have exalted yourself in the place of God. Do you not feel guilty about it? You have committed hundreds, thousands, doubtless millions of sins and are you so blind that you cannot remember them, or do you just refuse to think about them?

Your sins have made you a bad example to others. Think about how you have led others the wrong way by your deeds and actions. There are probably souls burning in hell right now, cursing you continually for having a part in sending them there. Your actions speak louder to others than your words. Have you never done anything or said anything which would cause others to stumble?

Meditate on what the Scriptures tell us that your sins deserve. You deserve to be cast into the unquenchable fires of hell where the damned shriek and wail continually in torment. If the cries of Korah, Dathan, and Abiram were enough to terrify the Israelites when the earth opened up and swallowed them alive (Number 16:31-34), then will you be so senseless as to ignore the cries of those now in hell? If the pit of hell were to be opened up and you could spend only one minute listening to the shrieks and curses of the damned in hell, you would fall on your knees before God and cry out for mercy.

Therefore plead with God to bring conviction to your heart for your sins. Beg Him to show you the depravity of your heart. Everything you do proceeds from corrupt motives and the polluted fountain of your own heart within. Ask Him to show you that clearly. Christ said, "For from within, out of the heart of men, proceed the evil thoughts, fornications, thefts, murders, adulteries, deeds of coveting and wickedness, as well as deceit, sensuality, envy, slander, pride, and foolishness. All these evil things proceed from within and defile the man" (Mark 7:21-23). Your corrupt heart is the source of your sin. That corrupt heart must be changed and regenerated by the power of the Holy Spirit or you will perish. "The heart is never soundly broken till thoroughly convinced of the heinousness of its original and deep-rooted depravity."[8] A clear sight of your sin should set you weeping and crying out to Christ for deliverance. You need to see yourself as a dead man and utterly lost before God so that you will seriously and diligently pursue salvation in Christ as you need to do.

Do not think that a few minutes considering your sins will avail you. You need to meditate on them daily to bring conviction to your hard heart. It is not very likely that five minutes with God will change your heart. He that never meditates on his sins is not likely to be broken-hearted for them, and broken-hearted you must be if you are to have life. "The sacrifices of God are a broken spirit; a broken and a contrite heart, O God, Thou wilt not despise" (Psalm 51:17). In his masterful work, *The Soul's Preparation for Christ,* Thomas Hooker wrote: "By serious meditation bring thy heart to such a loathing of sin, that it may never love it (any) more, besiege the heart with daily meditation, so that you may cut off any ease and refreshing that the heart may seem to have in any sinful course...It is not a 'Lord have mercy upon me,' and 'God forgive me,' that will serve the turn: No it is otherwise, if ever God set home this work, He will make you restless in seeking mercy, and nothing shall content you but mercy to pardon your sins, and grace to subdue them...Meditation brings all these sins, and miseries, and vileness, home to the heart, and the soul is made sensible by this means. Hold the heart there then, labour to keep the heart in the same temper, that it is brought into, by the consideration of sin...and therefore when thou settest thyself to muse and meditate upon thy corruptions, and lay them to heart; when thou findest thy soul to be affected with them, and humbled under them, labour then to see an absolute necessity of a Lord Jesus Christ, and so far see them, that they may drive thee, and compel thee to seek to Christ for mercy."[9] Be diligent. Be steadfast in seeking life. Begin at once using the means that God has provided for seeking Him. To aid you in this we will now examine those means in detail.

[1] Anthony Burgess, *Spiritual Refining,* (Ames, Iowa, International Outreach, Inc., 1990), p.p. 481 & 483. Reprint of the 1652 edition.
[2] William Whately, *The New Birth,* (London: Bernard Alsop, 1622), p. 15.
[3] Ibid, p. 101.
[4] Ibid, pp. 113-114.
[5] Jonathan Edwards, *The Works of Jonathan Edwards, Volume 1,* (London: Ball, Arnold, & Co., 1840), p. 671.
[6] Solomon Stoddard, *A Guide to Christ,* (Boston: J. Allen, 1714), p. 66.
[7] Thomas Watson, *The Doctrine of Repentance,* (Edinburgh: Banner of Truth Trust, 1987), p. 108.
[8] Joseph Alleine, *An Alarm to the Unconverted,* (London: Banner of Truth Trust, 1964), p. 104.
[9] Thomas Hooker, *The Soul's Preparation for Christ,* (London: M. F., 1640), pp. 164, 166, 171 & 230.

7

The Use of Holy Violence

*"The kingdom of heaven suffers violence, and
violent men take it by force" (Matthew 11:12).*

Diligence or what might be called a holy violence in using the means
that God has provided is necessarily implied in Christ's words about
the difficulty of getting into the kingdom of God and clearly stated in
such verses as Luke 13:24 and Matthew 11:12. Not that diligence in
seeking is meritorious in itself, but, as we will see, it is through these
means that God normally works to bring salvation to His people. In
numerous places the Lord Jesus spoke of the difficulty of getting into
the kingdom of God. "For the gate is small, and the way is narrow that
leads to life, and few are those who find it" (Matthew 7:14). "Strive to
enter by the narrow door, for many, I tell you, will seek to enter and will
not be able" (Luke 13:24). "The kingdom of heaven suffers violence,
and violent men take it by force" (Matthew 11:12). In these verses the
Lord tells us of the narrowness of the way and of the necessity to strive
in order to enter the kingdom of God. He speaks of men violently taking
the kingdom of God by force.

These expressions speak of a strength of desire and a firmness of
resolution possessed by those who make it their primary concern to
seek to obtain entrance to that kingdom. The obtaining of salvation is
the main concern and business of those who seek God in this way.
Jonathan Edwards wrote: "Besides desires after salvation, there should
be an earnest resolution in persons to pursue this good as much as lies
in their power...Those who are pressing into the kingdom of God, have
a disposition of heart to do everything that is required, and that lies in
their power to do, and to continue in it. They have not only earnestness,
but steadiness of resolution: they do not seek with a wavering, unsteady
heart, by turns or fits, being off and on; but it is the constant bent of their
soul, if possible to obtain the kingdom of God."[1]

Persons who are diligently seeking the kingdom are not that concerned with the difficulties which lie in their way. They are not worried
whether the way is easy or it is hard. The devil may attempt to discourage them by throwing doubts into their minds, but still they press
forward. This is the disposition of one who is striving to enter the
kingdom of God. "Such earnestness and thoroughness of endeavors, is

the ordinary means that God makes use of to bring persons to an acquaintance with themselves, to a sight of their own hearts, to a sense of their own helplessness, and to a despair in their own strength and righteousness. And such engagedness and constancy in seeking the kingdom of heaven, prepare the soul to receive it the more joyfully and thankfully, and the more highly to prize and value it when obtained. So that it is in mercy to us, as well as for the glory of His own name, that God has appointed such earnest seeking, to be the way in which He will bestow the kingdom of heaven."[2]

"It is possible that in the use of means we may arrive at happiness. Impossibility destroys endeavor: but here is a door of hope opened. The thing is feasible. It is not with us as with the damned in hell; there is a tombstone rolled over them. But while we are under the sound of Aaron's Bell, and the silver trumpet of the gospel is blown in our ears, while the Spirit of Grace breathes on us, and we are on this side of the grave; there is great hope...here is great encouragement to all to be serious and earnest in the matters of eternity, because they are yet in a capacity of mercy, no final sentence is already passed; God hath not taken up the drawbridge of mercy. Though the gate of paradise is straight, yet it is not shut. This should be as oil to the wheels, to make us lively and active in the business of salvation. Therefore as the husbandman plows in hope (James 5), so we should pray in hope; do all our work for heaven in hope, for the white flag of mercy is yet held forth."[3]

"When God bids us convert and turn, this is to show us what we ought to do, not what we can do. Yet let us do what we are able. We have power to avoid those rocks which will certainly ruin our souls; I mean gross sins. A man does not need to be in bad company; he does not need to swear or tell a lie; nor would he do it if it were by law death to swear an oath. We have power to cast ourselves upon the use of means: prayer, reading, holy conversation. This will condemn men at the last day that they did not act so vigorously in their sphere as they might have; they did not use the means and try whether God will give them grace. God will come with that soliciting question at last, 'Why didst not thou put my money to the exchangers? Why didst thou not improve that power which I gave thee?' Though we do not have the power to save ourselves, yet we must pursue after salvation."[4]

What then are the means which God has appointed which one can make use of to seek Him? The primary means are these: fervent prayer, reading and meditating on the word of God, and hearing the word of God preached. We will consider each one of these separately. Since these are God-ordained means by which a man may seek Him, they are very useful to you; however, they will only be successful, if the Holy Spirit attends them with His regenerating power.

First let us look at prayer and its relationship to the forsaking of sin. You must be willing to forsake all of your sins. It is not a little forsaking of some sins that will do. God demands that you forsake all sin if you are to have Christ. Therefore beg God to enable you to repent of all your sins in truth. Repentance and faith are both gifts from God. Beg the Spirit of God to change your heart and make you willing to turn away from all of your sins. Ask Him to regenerate you and make you holy. Beg Him to give you the gift of faith, that you might believe in the Lord Jesus Christ with all your heart. Ask Him to enable you to love Jesus Christ more than anyone or anything: to love Christ more than any other person, to love Christ more than your own self, and any material thing. Ask the Lord to enable you to surrender all you are and all you have to Jesus Christ as Lord. Christ is the Pearl of Great Price. You must be willing to give up all you have to get this pearl. Ask God to make your heart willing to forsake all the world for Christ.

Only if God chooses to have mercy on you will you be saved. Beg Him earnestly and fervently to have mercy on you. Ask Him repeatedly, over and over again. The Lord delights in being sought for His mercies. Let nothing hinder you or stand in your way of seeking salvation with all of the energy you have within you. Use the means of prayer as if your life depended on it. Beg the Lord to change your heart.

William Whately in the 17th century instructed men who were seeking salvation to "forget not in some manner of words to cry for this best of all gifts, and beg earnestly: and if thou canst not amplify, yet multiply; if thou canst not use variety of words, yet repeat the same request often, and again and again; if thine invention serve not to say more, let thy desire force thee to dwell upon this twenty times, and rather than fail, twice twenty times. O Lord, give unto me, a miserable sinner, Thy Spirit of life and grace to regenerate me."[5]

Asahel Nettleton illustrated the sinner's dependence upon God to give him a new heart this way: "Suppose a number of men are locked up in a room, playing cards. Some person informs them that the roof of the building is on fire, and that they must make their escape, or they will perish in the flames. Says one of them, 'We need not be in haste, we shall have time to finish the game.' 'But,' says the person who gave the alarm, 'your door is locked.' 'No matter for that,' he replies; 'I have the key in my pocket, and can open it at any moment.' 'But I tell you, that key will not open the door.' 'Won't it?' he exclaims; and rising from the table, flies to the door, and exerts himself to the utmost to open it. So sinners, while they believe that there is no difficulty in securing their salvation at any moment, quiet their consciences, and silence their fears. But when they are taught that such is the wickedness of their hearts, that they never will repent, unless God interposes by His regenerating grace; they are alarmed, and begin to inquire in deep distress what they shall do to be saved."[6]

Add to the means of fervent prayer, the reading and meditating upon the word of God. Read and study those verses which reveal both the law and the gospel to you. The law by itself will only terrify you and condemn you. The gospel without the law will breed presumption and false security. Strike a proper balance between the two so that you will be rightly convicted of your depravity and also see the way of deliverance provided for those who truly believe in Christ. First look upon those verses which tell you what you are like in your natural state without God. "The heart is deceitful above all things, and desperately wicked, who can know it?" (Jeremiah 17:9, KJV). "For all of us have become like one who is unclean, and all our righteous deeds are like a filthy garment" (Isaiah 64:6). "There is none righteous, not even one; there is none who understands, there is none who seeks for God; all have turned aside, together they have become useless; there is none who does good, there is not even one. Their throat is an open grave, with their tongues they keep deceiving, the poison of asps is under their lips; whose mouth is full of cursing and bitterness; their feet are swift to shed blood, destruction and misery are in their paths, and the path of peace have they not known. There is no fear of God before their eyes" (Romans 3:10-18).

Read and study those verses which reveal Christ and the gospel to you. Especially consider Isaiah 53:1-12 which tell of the death of Christ. Only faith in the shed blood of Jesus Christ can wash away your sins. Salvation is to be found only in Christ. He is the one mediator between God and men. Only Christ's righteousness applied to your life can justify you. Seek from the Lord that you may gain an interest in Christ's death. In the next section we will explore more fully why salvation is found only in Jesus Christ.

Study and meditate upon Psalm 51:1-17 as a pattern for begging for mercy. Recognize, as David acknowledges in verse 4, that your sin is fundamentally against God. You have offended His holiness and majesty: "Against Thee, Thee only, have I sinned, and done what is evil in Thy sight, so that Thou art justified when Thou dost speak, and blameless when Thou dost judge." David confesses his original depravity in verse 5: "Behold, I was brought forth in iniquity; and in sin my mother conceived me." He begs God for forgiveness repeatedly: "Wash me thoroughly from my iniquity, and cleanse me from my sin...Purify me with hyssop, and I shall be clean; wash me, and I shall be whiter than snow...Hide Thy face from my sins, and blot out all my iniquities. Create in me a clean heart, O God, and renew a steadfast spirit within me. Do not cast me away from Thy presence" (vs. 1, 7, & 9-11). He speaks about the only acceptable sacrifices to God, saying: "The sacrifices of God are a broken spirit; a broken and contrite heart, O God, Thou wilt not despise" (verse 17). If David, who was converted at the time he prayed this prayer, had need to pray such a prayer: how much more do you who are unconverted need to magnify and intensify these petitions. Apply this Psalm to your heart. Pray the words in it as your own.

Also notice the account of the Pharisee and the tax collector in Luke 18:9-14. The Pharisee was proud of himself. He was proud of his religious duties. His heart was not humble or broken before God. On the other hand, the tax collector was not even willing to look up to heaven for he knew of his unworthiness before God. He beat his breast to express sorrow and repentance. He begged God to have mercy on him. Christ commends the tax collector and says that the Lord justified him, not the Pharisee.

The leper who speaks with Christ in Luke 5:12-13 said to Him, "Lord, if You are willing, You can make me clean." This man begged the Lord to cleanse him, realizing that the Lord was free to do so or to refuse. If the Lord is willing, He can cleanse you also. Beg Him to do so, as the leper did.

The third means of grace to make use of is hearing the word of God preached. There is a great variety in the preaching of the word: some preaching is lively and convicting; much preaching, however, is apt to send men to hell resting on a bed of feathers. Seek out a place where the hard sayings of the Scriptures are plainly taught. At every opportunity go to hear the preaching of the Scriptures and meditate upon what you hear. "I confess that there is a kind of fine, neat, dainty preaching, consisting in well-sounding words, and strains of wit and human learning, to set out the skill and art of the speaker, and make the hearer applaud and commend him; which a man may well doubt, whether God will ever bless to the winning of souls."[7] Avoid such preaching! Go where the word of God is plainly and clearly taught, to a place where the preacher is not afraid to speak about sin and the need for repentance. Before you go to hear the preaching of God's word pray to the Lord that the Holy Spirit would bring home the message to your heart. Ask the Lord to use the word preached to reveal your sins and the wickedness of your heart to you, to reprove and rebuke you, and to instruct you, that the word may be profitable to your soul.

Do not undertake diligent seeking of God with time limitations fixed on your mind: that after a few hours or a few days of seeking you will have found God. Seek with the attitude that you are going to spend the rest of your life seeking if it is necessary. Do not set limits on God. He will act as He pleases, not according to your timetable. Jonathan Edwards, a man who saw the conversion of many hundreds of souls firsthand during the Great Awakening wrote: "Remember that if ever God bestows mercy upon you, He will use His sovereign pleasure about the time when. He will bestow it on some in a little time, and on others not till they have sought it long. If other persons are soon enlightened and comforted, while you remain long in darkness, there is no other way but for you to wait. God will act arbitrarily in this matter, and you cannot help it. You must even be content to wait, in a way of laborious and earnest striving, till His time comes. If you refuse, you will but undo yourself."[8]

Reverend Henry Scougal wrote in his work *The Life of God in the Soul of Man*, "To undertake vigorously, and rely confidently on the divine assistance, is more than half the conquest: 'Let us arise and be doing, and the Lord will be with us.' It is true, religion in the souls of men is the immediate work of God, and all our natural endeavors can neither produce it...nor merit those supernatural aids by which it must be wrought: the Holy Ghost must come upon us, and the power of the Highest must overshadow us, before that holy thing can be begotten, and Christ be formed in us: but yet we must not that this whole work should be done without any concurring endeavors of our own: we must not lie loitering in the ditch, and wait till Omnipotence pull us from thence; no, no! we must bestir ourselves, and actuate those powers which we have already received: we must put forth ourselves to our utmost capacities, and then we may hope that 'our labor shall not be in vain in the Lord'...It is true, that God hath been found of some who sought him not: he hath cast himself in their way, who were quite out of his...But certainly this is not God's ordinary method of dealing with men: though he hath not tied himself to means, yet he hath tied us to the use of them; and we never have reason to expect the divine assistance, than when we are doing our utmost endeavors."[9]

"Yet this caution I must necessarily insert: Though we shall not obtain the kingdom without violence, yet it shall also not be obtained for our violence. When we have done all, look up to Christ and free grace...though we are saved in the use of means, yet it is by grace. 'By grace ye are saved' (Ephesians 2:5). Heaven is a gift. 'It is your Father's good pleasure to give you the kingdom' (Luke 12:32). Why may one say, 'I have used violence for it; I have wrought for the kingdom.' Yes, but it is a gift that free grace bestows. We must look up to Christ for acceptance; not our sweat, but His blood saves."[10]

WHY IS SALVATION FOUND ONLY IN JESUS CHRIST?

Any seeking of God and salvation must be done through the Lord Jesus Christ. There is no salvation outside of Christ. The Lord Jesus told His followers: "I am the way, and the truth, and the life. No man comes to the Father, but by Me" (John 14:6). As Thomas Watson expressed it: It is not our sweat, but His blood that saves. It is important here that we briefly explore why salvation is found only in Jesus Christ. In doing this we will look at the necessity of a redeemer, the nature of the redeemer, and at redemption itself.

Man was created in the image of God, without sin or defect, as a responsible being capable of making moral choices. The first man, Adam, sinned against God by disobeying a direct command of God not to eat of the fruit of the tree of the knowledge of good and evil. "And the Lord God commanded the man, saying 'From any tree of the garden you may eat freely; but from the tree of the knowledge of good and evil you shall not eat, for in the day that you eat from it you shall surely die" (Genesis 2:16-17). How did man respond? By rejecting the authority of his Creator and going his own way; by taking from the tree which God had commanded him not to eat from and eating anyway. Adam and Eve sought to be autonomous, self-determining, seeking to decide for themselves what was good and what was evil, seeking to be their own rulers and governors, seeking to be their own gods.

What Adam did, all those he represented were also held responsible for. If Adam had obeyed, his obedience would have been transferred to all. Since Adam chose to disobey, all mankind fell with him and incurred the legal guilt of Adam's sin as their own. Thomas Manton wrote: "We saw the forbidden fruit with his eyes, gathered it with his hands, ate it with his mouth; that is, we were ruined by those things as though we had been there and consented to his acts."[11]

The penalty for sin was explained clearly to Adam before he sinned: death. The rest of Scripture confirms this as well. One example is found in Romans 6:23: "The wages of sin is death." This death is both physical (all men die because all are guilty of sin) and spiritual (all men are born spiritually dead and will suffer a second death in the lake of fire forever, if they are not redeemed). Death comes upon all men because all are charged with the legal guilt of Adam's sin. "Therefore, just as through one man (Adam) sin entered the world, and death through sin, and so death spread to all men, because all sinned" (Romans 5:12). "In Adam all die" (I Corinthians 15:22). Death is a judicial punishment passed upon all who, in God's eyes, are guilty of Adam's crime.

Man by his sin was delivered into the hands of Satan. Unregenerate or natural man is said to be "held captive" by the devil "to do his will" (II Timothy 2:26). The devil is said in Hebrews 2:14 to have "the power of death." Redemption thus involves not only pardon and forgiveness of sin, but deliverance as well. "The Lord, for our rebellions, being the supreme judge and governor, did, as it were, commit us, deliver us to Satan, leave us under the power of sin and the world. Satan, as the gaoler, leads us captive at his will; he makes use of sin and the world as fetters to increase and continue this misery. We could not be redeemed from this misery, but by a ransom."[12] Without a redeemer man is hopelessly lost because of sin and he will die and go to hell to receive the just punishment for his sin: everlasting torment. Thus the necessity of a redeemer is clearly demonstrated.

In exploring the nature of a redeemer we must first examine God's justice. God's justice in dealing with man's sin cannot be overturned. God must punish sin. He cannot remain righteous and at the same time overlook it. Payment must be made for every sin commited. Yet because sin has come to all men, no man is personally free from sin to be able to suffer the punishment necessary to redeem men from their sins. A sinner cannot redeem another sinner. Only God can accomplish such a redemption, but in order to do so, God must become a man, for only a man is capable of redeeming or buying back fallen men. This is what God did in the Person of Jesus Christ, the One who is both God and man. "Since then the children share in flesh and blood, He Himself likewise partook of the same, that through death He might render powerless him who had the power of death, that is, the devil; and might deliver those who through fear of death were subject to slavery all their lives" (Hebrews 2:14-15).

The Son of God became a man by being born of a virgin. The virgin birth was absolutely necessary so that Christ would not inherit Adam's corrupt nature. The redeemer of men must be free from original sin, otherwise He would be a sinner and could not qualify as a redeemer. God accomplished this through the Holy Spirit (Luke 1:35). The Holy Spirit overshadowed Mary and Jesus Christ was conceived in her womb, the Spirit also consecrating and purifying that part of her flesh where Christ was formed. Thus Christ entered the world free from sin.

It was also necessary that a redeemer be perfectly obedient to the law of God. God's law is immutable. It cannot be changed or altered. Penalty for disobedience is an essential part of that law. Christ came to fulfill the law through active obedience in doing all that it commanded and through passive obedience in suffering the penalty for its disobe-dience. Christ was said to be "born under the law in order that He might redeem those who were under the law" (Galatians 4:4-5). "For as through the one man's disobedience the many were made sinners, even so through the obedience of the One the many will be made righteous" (Romans 5:19). The law of God cannot save fallen men, for it can only condemn its violaters. Just one sin makes a man guilty and therefore subject to its curses and penalty (James 2:10). Jesus Christ came to fulfill the law in our place, not to relax its demands as many suppose.

Christ perfectly obeyed the law actively through His life. He also suffered the penalty and punishment of the law due to sinful men in His death. In doing that He fulfilled the just requirements of the law. Christ's death on the cross was for 1) the punishment of sins, 2) the price of redemption, and 3) a sacrifice for sins. Jesus Christ died to atone (make complete satisfaction to) God who was offended by man's sin, to divert the wrath of God, and to suffer the punishment due to sin by offering Himself as a substitutionary sacrifice for sins to appease God and bring about reconciliation to Him. For the sinner who avails himself of Christ's death this results in, among other things, the removal of guilt, the obtaining of forgiveness, and the prevention of the punishment that is deserved for sin.

The Scriptures make it very clear that the price of redemption is blood and it is only blood of an infinite value that can atone for sins committed against a holy, infinite God. "Without shedding of blood there is no forgiveness...so Christ also, having been offered once to bear the sins of many...has been manifested to put away sin by the sacrifice of Himself" (Hebrews 9:22, 28, & 26). Other Scriptures confirm that blood is the price of redemption: "For the life of the flesh is in the blood, and I have given it to you on the altar to make atonement for your souls; for it is the blood by reason of the life that makes atonement" (Leviticus 17:11). "In Him (Christ) we have redemption through His blood, the forgiveness of our trespasses" (Ephesians 1:7). "And not through the blood of goats and calves, but through His own blood, He entered the holy place once for all, having obtained eternal redemption" (Hebrews 9:12).

Jesus Christ died as a sacrifice for sins. In the substitutionary sacrifice of Jesus Christ, He (the sacrifice), took the place of the sinner. The offender deserved to be punished: Christ bore that punishment. The offender deserved to die: Christ died in the place of the one who had sinned. "For Christ also died for sins once for all, the just for the unjust, in order that He might bring us to God" (I Peter 3:18). God the Father has certified His acceptance of the death of Jesus Christ by raising Him from the dead. In Christ's sacrifice He tasted both the first and the second death for His children. Since Christ was God, His temporary sufferings were equivalent to the eternal sufferings men deserve for their sins. His sufferings for a time were of more weight and value than the eternal sufferings of sinners.

How amazing it is that God should do such a thing for sinners who were His enemies! David Clarkson expressed it this way: "How wonderful it is that God should become man, when man at his best estate is vanity...that He who gave life and being to all things, and sustains all in life and being by the word of His power, should die; that infinite glory should suffer a shameful death, should endure the cross, and despise the shame; that God blessed forever should become a curse, and die a cursed death, the death of accursed malefactors, hanging on a tree; that He who was God of all consolation, the fountain of all comfort and happiness, should expose Himself to the rage and cruelty of men, and the incensed wrath and justice of His Father; should suffer most exquisite pains and tortures in body and soul from men, and God too; the pains and sorrows both of the first and second death! That He who was the righteous lawgiver, the supreme judge, the almighty governor of the whole world, should not only suffer, but be punished in our stead, and bear the punishment of our crimes in His body too! That He who was more valuable than ten thousand worlds should give Himself a ransom for us, and not think His life, His blood dear, but lay it down freely as a price of our redemption from hell and wrath!"[13]
Behold the love of God in Christ for sinful men! Here is hope indeed! The only hope men have to be redeemed from sin, death, and hell is found in Jesus Christ. Can you see the beauty of such a Savior? Can you not submit to such a King as this or will you still choose to go your own way? If you refuse to surrender to Jesus Christ and continue on in your own ways, you remain God's enemy, subject to His wrath.

What then will you do? Reader, God has placed repentance from sin and faith in the Lord Jesus Christ as necessary conditions for obtaining life. Seeking God outside the Person of Jesus Christ will be a fruitless endeavor, doomed to failure, because no man can be saved apart from faith in the Lord Jesus. "Without faith it is impossible to please Him, for he who comes to God must believe that He is, and that He is a rewarder of those who seek Him" (Hebrews 11:6).

Oh, then seek that God might change your heart and make you willing to believe in Jesus Christ in truth. To mentally assent to the truths revealed in God's Holy Word about Jesus Christ is a necessary thing. To rest in mental assent as all that is necessary for salvation is a fatal error. Your great need is to be regenerated and have God impart true faith to you.

ENCOURAGEMENT TO ALL TO COME TO CHRIST

"And you will seek Me and find Me, when you search for Me with all your heart" (Jeremiah 29:13). "For if you cry for discernment, lift your voice for understanding; if you seek her as silver, and search for her as for hidden treasures; then you will discern the fear of the Lord, and discover the knowledge of God" (Proverbs 2:3-5). "Those who diligently seek Me will find Me" (Proverbs 8:17). Hear the promises of the Word of God, reader. And hearing them, determine to persevere through all difficulties in order to gain Christ.

If you would be violent in your pursuit of salvation, then keep heaven continually in your mind. Every time you look up at the sky, let it be a reminder to you that eternity is real and that above the starry heaven is the heaven of heavens, the dwelling place of God and those who love Him. "Just as it is written, 'Things which eye has not seen and ear has not heard, and which have not entered the heart of man, all that God has prepared for those who love Him'" (I Corinthians 2:9). "If the mountains were gold; if every sand of the sea were a diamond; if the whole globe were a shining chrysolite, it were infinitely beneath the glory of this kingdom."[14] The kingdom of heaven is offered to men by the God who made them. Are the pleasures of the world to be preferred before the glories of the kingdom of heaven? Seeking God with all your heart is difficult, but is it any more difficult than lying in hell to all eternity? Do those now in hell have any delight and enjoyment in their past sins? What do you think they would give now for the opportunity you have to seek God? You have plenty of time now to take care of your body, to eat and to sleep: do you have no time for your eternal soul? If an earthly kingdom were offered to you, would you simply ignore it? Why then do you think nothing of an eternal, heavenly kingdom offered to you, not by man, but by the God of the universe?

Let us look at several accounts recorded in the Scriptures of those who sought Christ. The example of the Canaanite woman is given to us as one of determined perseverance. In Matthew 15:21-28 her story is recorded. When she first cried to the Lord to have mercy on her, Christ did not answer her, even though she called Him, "Lord, Son of David." She kept on begging so much that the disciples began asking Christ to send her away. The Lord's response to His disciples is not one which would normally give a person great hope: "I was sent only to the lost sheep of the house of Israel" (Matthew 15:24). But the woman would not let the doctrine of election discourage her. Even though she might not be among the chosen ones, she perseveres still. She prays more earnestly, bowing down and worshiping Christ and crying out, "Lord, help me!" Still Christ turns her away saying, "It is not good to take the children's bread, and throw it to the dogs" (Matthew 15:26). How does she respond? By humbling herself even more and acknowledging Christ's words about her to be true. She says in effect, "Yes, Lord, you are right in what you say. I don't deserve anything from you, but give me of your mercy anyway." To which He responds, "O woman, your faith is great; be it done for you as you wish" (Matthew 15:28).

Read the account of a blind man named Bartimaeus in Luke 18:35-43: "And it came about that as He was approaching Jericho, a certain blind man was sitting by the road, begging. Now hearing a multitude going by, he began to inquire what this might be. And they told him that Jesus of Nazareth was passing by. And he called out, saying, 'Jesus, Son of David, have mercy on me!' And those who led the way were sternly telling him to be quiet, but he kept crying out all the more, 'Son of David, have mercy on me.' And Jesus stopped and commanded that he to be brought to Him; and when he had come near, He questioned him. 'What do you want Me to do to you?' And he said, 'Lord, I want to regain my sight.' And Jesus said to him, 'Receive your sight; your faith has made you well.' And immediately he regained his sight, and began following Him, glorifying God; and when all the people saw it, they gave praise to God."

Bartimaeus went to the right person, Jesus Christ. He cried out to Christ for mercy. Those around him were disturbed by his outcries, but that did not stop him. Satan will be disturbed by your seeking of God and seek to cast discouragements in your way. Persevere still. Bartimaeus, instead of being discouraged, cried out all the more. "Son of David, have mercy on me." Bartimaeus received the fruit of his request from the hand of Christ, purely as a gift of His mercy.

Determine to persevere through all difficulties in order to find Christ. Jacob stands forth as a shining example in the Old Testament of one determined to receive the blessing of God. When Jacob wrestled all night with the Angel of the Lord as daybreak came Jacob cried out, "I will not let you go unless you bless me" (Genesis 32:26). You do the same. Refuse to quit besieging heaven with your prayers and petitions until God answers you.

Charles Haddon Spurgeon speaking of this striving, wrote in a sermon entitled *Holy Violence,* what follows. In it Spurgeon portrays a dialogue between a man who is striving for the kingdom and one who does not see such striving as necessary: "No man ever gets peace until he gets into such a passion of earnestness to be saved, that he cannot find peace until Christ speaks pardon to his soul, and brings him into life and liberty. 'The kingdom of heaven suffereth violence, and the violent take it by force.'...Ask one such man, again, why is he so violent in prayer; he replies, 'Ah, I know the value of the mercy I receive. Why, I am asking for pardon, for heaven, for eternal life, and am I to get these with a few yawns and sleepy prayers?...No, my God; if thou wouldst make me tarry a hundred years, and sigh, and groan, and cry through that long century; yes, if I might but have heaven at last, all my prayers would have been well-spent; nay, had they been a thousand times as many, they were well rewarded if thou wouldst hear me at last. But,' he says again, 'if you want to know why I am so earnest, let me tell you it is because I cannot bear to be lost forever.' Hear the earnest sinner when he speaks. You say to him, 'Why so earnest?' The tear is in his eye, the flush is on his cheek, there is emotion in every feature, while he says, 'Would to God I could be far more earnest; do you know that I am a lost soul, perhaps before another hour is over I may be shut up in the hopeless fires of hell! Oh, God, have mercy on me, for if thou dost not, how terrible is my fate. I shall be lost—lost forever!'"[15]

Come to Christ now. Do not delay. He is the only One who can save you. "May I come without leaving my sins?" No. Forsake your sins and come freely (Luke 13:3). "May I come while I am still in love with the world?" No. Forsake your love of the world and be loosed of that wretched burden to your soul. You cannot love the world and have Christ, too (I John 2:15). "May I come and still live for myself and yet escape the damnation of hell?" He who lives to please himself does not come rightly and shall not find life (Luke 9:23-25). He who comes only to escape the damnation of hell has no true love to God (Acts 8:21). Forsake your sins and accept life on the Lord's terms! Come! "And the Spirit and the bride say, 'Come.' And let the one that hears say, 'Come.' And let the one that is thirsty come; and let the one who wishes take the water of life without cost" (Revelation 22:17). "You have answered my other questions, but that verse seems to say that I might come without cost." Yes, you may, but the cost referred to here does not mean that you need not give up anything, but that you cannot do anything to pay for or contribute to your own salvation. Poverty in no way hinders a man's coming to Christ. The poor are just as welcome to come as the rich. Those without money are accepted just as freely as those who have much. "Ho! Everyone who thirsts, come to the waters; and you who have no money come, buy and eat" (Isaiah 55:1).

When we forsake all for Christ, we do not give to God any price for Him. We only rid ourselves of those things which would hinder our freely coming to Him. "If one should offer me handfuls of gold, I for the present having my hands full of clay, I should quickly be rid of the clay that I may finger the gold, yet I do not pay for the gold with the clay but only prepare myself to receive it."[16] God turns away no one because they cannot give, but only because they will not give what God requires. God expects from us whatever we have, whether it be little or much. God asks you for your sins, your selfish desires, your love of the world, your life. Yet all of these are worth nothing compared to the glorious person of the Lord Jesus Christ and the heavenly riches He offers to those who come to Him in faith. Repent of your sins. Come to Christ. Do not delay. "'I have no pleasure in the death of anyone that dies,' says the Lord God.'Therefore repent and live'" (Ezekiel 18:32).

Puritan Thomas Hooker wrote of the response of the people of Ninevah when God threatened judgment upon them for their sins: "The people of Ninevah said, 'Who knows but God may repent?' This upheld their hearts, and made them seek to the Lord in the use of means, and the Lord had mercy on them...So hope provokes the soul to use the means, and say, I am a damned man, but if there be any hope, I will pray, and hear, and fast; Who knows but God may show mercy to my poor soul."[17] Be encouraged, therefore, to persevere diligently with every ounce of strength within you. Pastor L. R. Shelton, Jr., has written: "There must be no pretense about seeking Him. If you desire to be saved, there must be no playing and trifling and half-heartedness with Him. The search must be real...earnest and intense or it will be a failure. Half-hearted seeking is no seeking at all."[18] "Seek the Lord while He may be found, call upon Him while He is near" (Isaiah 55:6).

The time has come for me to close. What else can I say? Oh, Lord, let these words not fall upon deaf ears! Reader, hear the prayer of a humble servant of God, Joseph Alleine, recorded over 300 years ago, for his words echo my thoughts and prayers better than I can express them. Hear him as he prays to the Lord on your behalf: "*Let the tempter not hinder him* (the reader) *in delays. Let him not stir from this place, nor take his eyes from these lines, till he resolve to forego his sins, and accept life on Thy self-denying terms. In Thy Name, O Lord God, did I go forth to these labours; in Thy Name do I close them. Let not all the time they have cost be lost hours; let not all the thoughts of the heart, and all the pains that have been about them be lost labour. Lord, put Thy hand upon the heart of this reader, and send Thy Spirit, as once Thou didst Philip to join himself to the chariot of the eunuch while he was reading the Word. And though I should never know it while I live, yet I beseech Thee, O Lord God, let it be found at the last day that some souls are converted by these labours; and let some be able to stand forth and say that by these persuasions they were won unto Thee. Amen, Amen.* Let him that readeth say, Amen."[19]

[1] Jonathan Edwards, *The Works of Jonathan Edwards, Volume 1,* (London: Ball, Arnold, & Co., 1840), p. 655.

[2] Ibid, pp. 656-657.

[3] Thomas Watson, *Heaven Taken by Storm,* (London: R. W. for Thomas Parkhurst, 1670), pp. 135-136.

[4] Thomas Watson, *Heaven Taken by Storm,* (Ligonier, PA: Soli Deo Gloria, 1992), p. 65.

[5] William Whately, *The New Birth,* (London: Bernard Alsop, 1622), p. 122.

[6] Bennet Tyler, *Memoir of the Life and Character of Rev. Asahel Nettleton, D.D.,* (Hartford: Robins & Smith, 1844), p. 328.

[7] William Whately, *The New Birth,* (London: Bernard Alsop, 1622), p. 129.

[8] Jonathan Edwards, *The Works of Jonathan Edwards, Volume 1,* (London: Ball, Arnold, & Co., 1840), p. 658.

[9] Reverend Henry Scougal, *The Life of God in the Soul of Man,* (Harrisonburg, VA: Sprinkle Publications, 1986), pp. 92-94.

[10] Thomas Watson, *Heaven Taken by Storm,* (Ligonier, PA: Soli Deo Gloria, 1992), pp. 86-87.

[11] Thomas Manton, quoted by A. W. Pink, *Gleanings from the Scriptures: Man's Total Depravity,* (Chicago: Moody Press, 1969), p. 39.

[12] David Clarkson, *The Works of David Clarkson, Volume 3,* (Edinburgh: Banner of Truth, 1988), p. 70.

[13] Ibid, p. 77.

[14] Thomas Watson, *Heaven Taken by Storm,* (London: R. W. for Thomas Parkhurst, 1670), pp. 144-145.

[15] Charles Haddon Spurgeon, *The New Park Street Pulpit, Volume 5,* (Grand Rapids: Baker Book House, 1990), pp. 219 & 221.

[16] William Pink, *The Trial of a Christian's Sincere Love Unto Christ,* (Oxford: L. Lichfield, 1657), p. 210.

[17] Thomas Hooker, *The Soul's Preparation for Christ,* (London: M. F., 1640), pp. 311 & 316.

[18] L. R. Shelton, Jr., *Christ and the Seeking Soul,* (Pensacola, FL: Mt. Zion Bible Church, nd), p. 4.

[19] Joseph Alleine, *An Alarm to the Unconverted,* (London: Banner of Truth Trust, 1964), p. 148.

THE END

Appendix

The Gospel & Martyrdom

*"If anyone comes to Me, and does not hate his own father
and mother and wife and children and brothers and sisters,
yes, and even his own life, he cannot be
My disciple" (Luke 14:26).*

The gospel and martyrdom: what do these two have in common, if anything? Is one in any way related to the other? Most gospel preaching in today's churches, even evangelical churches, would be horrified at the thought of any connection between the two. The popular gospel of today suggests that Christian belief is easy. "Just believe and receive Christ" is the common theme of most evangelistic efforts. What does martyrdom have to do with that?

Rather than examining the message of today, it would be much wiser for us to examine the Scriptures themselves to see what they say about these two seemingly separate issues. A simple examination of a few selected texts which use the word "believe" will not be sufficient for this type of inquiry, for the Bible must be taken in its entirety, not piecemeal. Nor does it go along with sound biblical interpretation to simply say, "Believe means believe doesn't it? How could it be easier than that?"

The Lord Jesus Christ is the definer of the gospel message, not modern theologians. The issue of what it means to believe must rest with how Jesus defines commitment to Himself. If Christ links the gospel message and martyrdom then we must be willing to listen and change our position, not attempt to redefine His words for Him to fit our preconceived ideas of the gospel.

Even a cursory examination will clearly show us that the word "believe" means much more than to agree with a few facts about ourselves and the death of Christ. James tells us: "You believe that God is one. You do well; the demons also believe, and shudder" (James 2:19). James is clearly speaking of a type of belief that a man may have which is not saving and will not avail to eternal life. A. W. Pink has written, "It is one thing to really think we believe a thing, it is quite another to actually do so...In temporal affairs what a man really believes is best ascribed by his practice. Suppose I meet a traveller in a narrow gorge and tell him that just ahead is an unpassable river, and that the bridge across it is rotten: if he declines to turn back, am I not warranted in concluding that he does not believe me?"[1] What Pink says here applies directly to what we will examine in relation to the words of Christ about being one of His followers. What we really believe is born out by our practice.

WHAT DID CHRIST SAY ABOUT COMMITMENT?

Is there anywhere in the gospels where the Lord Jesus clearly defines the terms by which one could measure whether or not he was a true follower of Christ or not? Does the Lord define commitment for us? Yes, there are, in fact, several places. One is found in Luke 14:25-33, where it is said in verses 25-26: "Now great multitudes were going along with Him; and He turned and said to them, 'If anyone comes to Me, and does not hate his own father and mother and wife and children and brothers and sisters, yes, and even his own life, he cannot be My disciple.'"

Great multitudes were following the Lord. No doubt many reasons and motives were represented by these multitudes. Christ was aware of their reasons and motives. Therefore, so that those following Christ might not dishonor Him and deceive themselves by absurd and foolish ideas of the easiness for them to obtain whatever good could be gotten from Him by their lip service to Him, the Lord thought it wise to let them know beforehand what they must resolve on if they were to follow Him unto salvation. Christ lays before them the terms of His offer of salvation. His terms are these: If anyone wishes to be a true follower of Christ and share in His kingdom, he must love Jesus Christ more than any other person or thing in this world, and even more than life itself. Any commitment that falls short of this disqualifies a person from being a follower of Christ.

"Surely this cannot be so!" you exclaim. "I have always heard that it was easy to be a follower of Jesus." Then what you have heard was wrong. Richard Baxter comments on such a reaction in his *Treatise on Self-Denial* saying, "God forbid, say they, that none should be Christians and be saved, but those that thus deny themselves, and take up their cross and forsake all they have, and accept not life itself from Christ. They say they believe in Christ, and yet they say, God forbid his word should be true; or, God forbid we should believe Christ hath spoken this in His gospel! See what kind of Christians multitudes are! Every man and woman on earth that take themselves for true Christians, and do not deny themselves for life and all, for the sake of Christ and the hope of everlasting glory, are mere self-deceivers, and no true Christians at all...But I beseech you, remember that this is the lowest degree of self-denial that is saving, to set more by Christ and the hopes of glory, than by all this world and life itself; and to be habitually resolved to forsake life and all, rather than to forsake Him. No less than this is proper self-denial, or will prove you Christians and in a state of life."[2]

Is this what it means to hate one's life? Not to count anything so dear as you would not be willing to part with it for the sake of following and obeying Christ? To value Christ above all human relationships? To value Christ above all material things? To value Christ above even our very lives? Is this what the gospel is all about? *Yes it is.*

The hatred the Lord Jesus speaks of here (Luke 14:26), is more a passive than an active hatred. It is a disesteem of those things which our nature might lawfully value highly, when they conflict, compete, or hinder in any way our serving Christ or glorifying Him. To forsake quickly that which might normally be so dear to us for the sake of Christ that to on-lookers it would seem like hate because we so readily forsake it (or them); doing as Abraham did when he willingly offered up Isaac as a sacrifice; doing as Moses did when he "refused to be called the son of Pharaoh's daughter...Considering the reproach of Christ greater riches than the treasures of Egypt" (Hebrews 11:25 & 27); and included in that passive hatred is "yes, even your own life."

Other Scriptures bear this out. In Luke 9:23-25 it says: "And He was saying to them all, 'If anyone wishes to come after Me, let him deny himself, and take up his cross daily and follow Me. For whosoever wishes to save his life shall lose it, but whoever loses his life for My sake, he is the one who will save it. For what is a man profited if he gains the whole world, and loses or forfeits himself?'"

The Lord Jesus is talking about coming after Him, about a man losing his eternal soul if he does not deny himself and take up His cross. What does this mean? What did a cross represent in the time of Jesus Christ? It meant only one thing—a cross was an instrument of extreme torture, pain, and death. Christ is calling for total self-denial, a total renouncing of living to please self and engaging in selfish pursuits, even to the point of willingly giving one's life for Christ. It is counting the cause of Christ to be more precious than anything else in life and being willing to sacrifice one's very being for His sake. It is a total surrender to the Lordship and authority of Jesus Christ over my life. This and this alone is true salvation.

What does Christ mean when He says, "Whosover wishes to save his life shall lose it"? A man may save his life by keeping it for himself; by following his own way; by doing his own thing. A man may profess his love to God and Christ, but not exhibit the least degree of self-denial for Him. The one who does that is not saved.

A man may do great works, seemingly for Christ, but all the while, in hidden thoughts and motives, be serving himself. The one who seeks to keep his own life for himself in this way will lose his eternal soul. Only the one who willingly forsakes all for Christ, even to the point of giving up his life will save his life eternally.

David Clarkson has written: "If your hearts cannot say as the apostle, 'Neither count I my life dear, that I may win Christ' (Acts 20:24); I am not only ready to be bound, but, (Acts 24:13), to die, whenever and wherever He shall require it; not only ready to sacrifice my name and reputation, but my person for Christ...not only ready to part with relations, liberty, country, enjoyments, but to part with my life whenever he calls for it;—if this be not the resolution of your hearts, you are not His disciples; for this He requires of all (Luke 14:26), 'He that does not hate his life,' i.e. is not as free to part with it for Christ as if he hated it, he loves his life more than Christ; and He (Christ) will never count them Christians, whatever they may count themselves, who love anything, though it be life itself, more than Him, or equally with Him."[3]

Even in the same chapter of Luke we see this affirmed by Jesus. "But, Jesus said to him, 'No one, after putting his head to the plow and looking back, is fit for the kingdom of God" (Luke 9:62). Who is it in the Scriptures who is infamous for looking back? Lot's wife. She stands as an eternal memorial to those who love the world and their own lives more than Christ. Christ even uses her as an example to warn us: "Remember Lot's wife. Whoever seeks to keep his life shall lose it, and whoever loses his life shall preserve it alive" (Luke 17:32-33).

J. C. Ryle wrote in his classic work *Holiness:* "I do urge on every professing Christian who wishes to be happy, the immense importance of making no compromise between God and the world. Do not try to drive a hard bargain, as if you wanted to give Christ as little of your heart as possible, and to keep as much as possible of the things of this life. Beware lest you overreach yourself, and end by losing all. Love Christ with all your heart and mind and soul and strength. Seek first the kingdom of God, and believe that then all other things shall be added to you. Take heed that you do not prove a copy of the character John Bunyan draws, Mr. Facing-both-ways. For your happiness' sake, for your usefulness' sake, for your safety's sake, for your soul's sake, beware of the sin of Lot's wife."[4]

The Lord Jesus also spoke of a time when, "they will deliver you up to tribulation, and will kill you, and you will be hated by all nations on account of My name. And at that time many will fall away and will betray one another and hate one another. And many false prophets will arise and deceive many...But the one who endures to the end, it is he who will be saved" (Matthew 24:9-11 & 13). I am not interested in trying to pinpoint a time when this was or will be fulfilled. I *am* interested in observing the connection between persecution and falling away (apostasy).

Christ speaks of a time of great persecution when "they will kill you...on account of My name." Immediately after a description of this persecution He talks about apostatizing or falling away from the faith. He then says that "the one who endures to the end...shall be saved." The strong implication here in Christ's teaching is that, in relation to the time spoken about, it is *only* the one who is willing to endure this intense persecution without denying Him or falling away who will be saved: they and they alone. Those who fall away from the faith due to persecution were never saved to begin with. Their faith was not real. So it is in every age.

The book of Hebrews echos the same truth in chapter 10 verses 38-39: "But My righteous one shall live by faith; and if he shrinks back, My soul has no pleasure in him. But we are not of those who shrink back to destruction, but of those who have faith to the preserving of the soul." The one who shrinks back from enduring persecution for Christ shrinks back to destruction or to put it more plainly, hell. God has *no pleasure* in such a person. Such a person does not act in faith or live by faith. Therefore, they are not one of God's children. Their faith is the wrong kind. It is not faith unto the "preserving of the soul."

Other Scriptures affirm Christ's words regarding the necessity of loving Him above all else as necessary to salvation. Deuteronomy 6:5 says, "And you shall love the Lord you God with all your heart, and with all your soul and with all you might." Consider this, can a person truly be said to love God with all of their heart if they love their lives more than God? Does loving God with all of our hearts mean that we are free to deny Christ anytime our persons are threatened and at the same time still consider ourselves good Christians?

Others spoken of in the book of Revelation are said to have overcome (language which implies perseverance to the end and eternal salvation) because "of the blood of the Lamb and because of the word of their testimony, and they did not love their life even to death" (Revelation 12:11). Such are the characteristics of all who follow the Lord Jesus in truth. Christ's words are clear to those who have ears to hear them. So is the demand of God in Deuteronomy 6:5. God's standards have not been lowered or changed in any way. He still demands all of our hearts if we are to be His followers in truth, even if it means the loss of our lives for Him. Anything less than this is not the type of faith which God gives to His children. God gives faith which perseveres and endures to the end, no matter what the cost.

DOES A WILLINGNESS TO DIE FOR CHRIST PROVE THAT A MAN IS GODLY?

Is there any external action which a person may do which would give positive evidence that such a person was truly saved? Does a willingness to die for the sake of Christ prove that a man is godly and has genuine biblical faith? Surely, if anything were an indicator of faith this would be it, wouldn't it? How could a person who gave his life for the cause of Christ be immediately transported into the depths of hell and there spend eternity in torment with blasphemers and persecuters of Christ? It seems hard to believe that such a thing is possible and yet the Scriptures indicate it is.

Paul wrote these words to the Corinthians: "And if I give all my possessions to feed the poor, and if I deliver my body to be burned, but do not have love, it profits me nothing" (I Corinthians 13:3). There are two amazing truths conveyed in this verse. First, that a man may sell all that he owns and use the money to feed the poor; that he might engage in extraordinary works of mercy to the poor and downtrodden in the name of Christ and still not be a true believer. And secondly, that a man may willingly die and give his body to be burned in the fire, supposedly for the sake of Christ, and yet go to hell and burn there eternally as well.

If Scripture did not put forth such a doctrine, I would not declare it; but, when Scripture does so, I must as well. The marrow of Christianity is found in the motives of the heart. Thus an external action may appear outwardly good, but if it proceeds from corrupt motives, that action, from God's perspective, is evil. Thus, it is very possible for a man to suffer much loss and endure much hardship in the name of Christ and not have his heart sound toward God. Anthony Burgess wrote in his great work *Spiritual Refining:* "We may see this fully confirmed in a parallel about giving alms, and relieving the poor. There is scarce any religious duty that has more promises made to it in Scripture than this has, yet a Pharisee who frequently gave alms, could take no comfort at all from those promises because his motives were carnal and unworthy. Thus in sufferings for Christ, even in imprisonments, and death itself, it being possible that corrupt grounds may sway us as well as heavenly, there can be no solid comfort from such external sufferings, though never so sad or miserable. Therefore no promise of heaven is made to the most specious external exercise of any religious action whatso-ever."[5]

Many false reasons and motives may cause a man to be willing to suffer for Christ. A man may suffer for the truth, or for a good cause, not because it is true or good, but because it is *his* cause. Socrates died for the truth that there was only one god, which shows us that a man unrenewed and unregenerated, may die for truths he is convinced about.

Pride and vain glory may cause a man to do much in the name of Christ when actually he is doing it for his own profit. A man may desire to make for himself a name and to be thought great in the eyes of the world so that future generations will praise him and becoming a martyr may be the best way to achieve this goal. Unregenerate man's actions all end in self, no matter how religious they are.

Stoutness of heart and spirit and a desire to prove how tough they are often causes men to do strange things. Again self and self-love are what is really behind such boldness. A willingness to suffer can come directly from the Spirit of God, but also from the strength in a man's own spirit.

Likewise, a man may be misguided in his own heart and conscience as to what the truth is and yet be willing to die for his mistaken judgments and opinions. Many heretics throughout history have been willing to die for their causes. "Herein we delude ourselves, because we judge our estate good, by external actions, when yet reprobates may do the like...Do the godly pray? Hear? So do the reprobates. May the godly suffer, be imprisoned, die for the truth? So may reprobates."[6] There-fore, no man may judge himself to be a Christian by any external deed whatsoever, no matter how glorious it may seem.

OBJECTIONS CONSIDERED

Certainly, what has been said thus far does not agree with much liberal or even evangelical teaching today. It is important to consider some of the more common objections which men are apt to raise against this teaching. We will consider the two main objections which are among the most often repeated:
1) Isn't this teaching only for higher level believers? 2) May I not love one thing more than or at least equal to Christ?

Isn't This Teaching Only For Higher Level Believers?

This is perhaps the most common objection used today. There are those who say that to be a believer is one thing and a disciple another; that the two may be separate and distinct. To them a believer is one who has accepted Jesus as their personal Saviour and a disciple is one who has surrendered to Jesus as their Lord. To make this claim does great injustice to a literal interpretation of not only this text (Luke 14:25-33), but also many others as well. It also does great injury to the Person of the Lord Jesus as well as His gospel.

It should be clear to all from the context set by the writer in Luke 14:25-26 that Jesus is not speaking to only a few selected individuals. In verse 25 Luke speaks of great multitudes to whom the Lord Jesus addresses this discourse. Does anyone imagine that the multitudes were saved? Christ makes it clear in many places that few will be saved, saying such things as, "Strive to enter by the narrow door; for many, I tell you, will seek to enter and will not be able" (Luke 13:24). As if this were not enough, in verse 26, the Lord uses the words, "if anyone comes to Me and does not..." This is equivalent to "if any of you individually." This is further clarified in verse 33 where Jesus says, "therefore no one of you can be My disciple who does not give up all his own possessions." Christ is speaking to the multitude as individuals and giving them a gospel invitation.

Those who claim the word disciple means something other than "Christian" need to study the use of the word "disciple" in the Scriptures. We will look at two such usages to illustrate our point. In the Book of Acts (also written by Luke) the word "disciple" occurs numerous times. Acts 14:19-21 presents us with a very clear example of what is meant by the term: "But Jews came from Antioch and Iconium, and having won over the multitudes, they stoned Paul and dragged him out of the city, supposing him to be dead. But while the disciples stood around him, he arose and entered the city. And the next day he went away with Barnabus to Derbe. And after they had preached the gospel to that city and had made many disciples, they returned to Lystra and to Iconium and to Antioch."

First, we must ask whether someone supposes this was a special group of higher level believers who stood around Paul after he had been stoned by the Jews? Is this what is meant or are these simply believers? Verse 21 should make it clear that this is not what is meant here, for there we are plainly told that the preaching of the gospel in that city resulted in many becoming disciples. Let me repeat that: the preaching of the gospel resulted in disciples being made! How then can "disciples" be anything other than "believers"?

Acts 11 tells of Barnabus' journey and preaching in Antioch where he was used of God to bring considerable numbers to the Lord.

Barnabus goes to Tarsus in search of Saul to help him in this effort and in verse 26 it is said, "the *disciples* were first called *Christians* in Antioch." How much plainer could it be stated? Disciple...Christian– – there is no difference. All true Christians are disciples no matter how old in the faith they are. Although further texts could be cited, if one will not believe the plain words of Jesus in Luke 14:25-33, how would other texts convince them? One who remains unconvinced by the words of Jesus Christ demonstrates at the very least that his own prejudices and preconceived notions have hindered his ability to rightly understand the Word of God.

May I Not Love One Thing More Than Christ or at Least Equal to Christ?

This objection is made by those who know they love something more than Christ, but who still want to be counted among His followers. They are headed for hell, but they do not want to admit it. They want the world and Christ, too. If a man sees no extraordinary excellency in Christ, then he just holds fast to what he has. If he is blind to the superlative worth of Christ then his affections will continue glued to the trash and muck of the world.

A man who is confronted with the true gospel may think: "The things offered by Christ are excellent things, but they are offered on such difficult terms, therefore, maybe for today other things may be better for me; so I will make the most for myself that I can today and think on eternity later and hope that God's mercy will be with me in the time of death." Such a man shows by his attitude that he is unworthy of Christ and true riches.† Why should God prostitute His treasures before the trampling of such swine? Would a man give a tiny child diamonds to play with when the child is just as satisfied with a sand pile? Certainly not! He would be a fool to do so. God is not a fool, moreover, His justice would not allow such an inequity to exist by giving salvation to someone who loves something more than Christ. Would you believe a man who said he greatly esteemed a pearl when he would much rather have a kernal of corn instead? Thus any man who esteems something more than Christ infinitely devalues the mercies of God in Christ and

---

† "The ungodly reckon upon being religious tomorrow, and therefore put off repentance, forsaking the world, and living for eternity, to some infinitely future day...Our intense anxiety about earthly, and apathy about heavenly things, speak but too plainly. The young look to middle age; the more advanced to the last stage of life." Charles Bridges, *Proverbs,* p. 500.

shows that he really does not esteem Christ at all; for the love of Christ is an infinitely greater treasure than anything this world or all that is in it can offer.

If a man loves any one thing in the world more than Christ, he does Christ as much dishonor as the one who never shows the least bit of interest in Christ. Would a woman believe a man to be sincere who told her repeatedly of his love for her, when she knew that he also slept with other women? Would a husband be pleased that his wife loved him more than a million other men, if she loved just one other man more than he? Will God accept lip service to Him when the heart is given to love other things more than Him? The riches of the world are trash compared to the glorious Lord of the universe. Paul said that he counted all things as dung in comparison to Christ (Philippians 3:8). If we love anything more than Christ, that one thing may force us to betray Him just as wickedly as if we loved one hundred things better. The one who loves one thing more than Christ will be quickly persuaded, under the right circumstances, to love other things more as well.

Can a man love any one thing equal to Christ and be His follower? This may sound reasonable, but in reality it is an impossible proposition. The Lord Jesus Himself has said that no man can serve two masters "for either he will hate the one and love the other, or he will hold to the one and despise the other" (Matthew 6:24). Loving Christ chiefly for salvation and benefits is a mercenary love. Mercenary motives are unacceptable to God. It is like the wife who loves her husband only for his money. She does not really love her husband; she loves what she can get out of him. She uses him for her own selfish purposes.

"He therefore that would certainly know how much he loves his blessed Saviour, that would judge exactly of the measure of his love unto Him, must not do it by feeling the pulse, as it were, or calculating the degrees of his affections to Him; but by comparing his affections unto Christ with his affections to other matters."[7] This Christ plainly asks the multitude to do in Luke 14:25-33, just as He challenged the rich young ruler to do this when He told him to sell all he had, give it to the poor, and follow Him. The man quickly realized what he valued most and it wasn't Christ. He went away very sorrowful, for he knew that eternal life had eluded him. The one who professes to love Christ and to be His follower cannot love anything more than or equal to Christ, even his own life, or he is not a Christian. Christ told us that the one who loves something more than He "is not worthy" of Him (Matthew 10:38).

HOW DO WE APPLY THIS DOCTRINE?

Natural men are likely to rebel against this doctrine and think that it is too difficult a demand for Christ to make. They might consent that it would be a commendable thing if a man was willing to die for Christ, but that it is something which only a few saints ever attain. They do not want to believe that this is the lowest measure of saving grace that a man may have and be saved. Richard Baxter addressed this very issue over three hundred years ago, saying: "Whether you love an immortal, holy life with God, or this earthly, fleshly life better, is the great question on which it will be resolved whether you are Christians or infidels at the heart, and whether you are heirs of heaven or hell...yet it goeth very hardly down with them that it should be the lowest measure of saving grace, and that the weakest Christian must have it that will be saved: for, they say, what can the strongest do more than die for Christ? But to this I answer, 1) There is no room for objections against so plain a word of God. It is the wisdom of God, and not our reason, (which) must determine by what we shall attain it. And if God say plainly, that 'if any man come to Christ, and hate not his own life, (that is, love it not so much less than Christ, that for His sake he can use it as a hated thing is used), he cannot be My disciple,' (Luke 14:26); it is too late for the vote of man, or all the clamour of foolish reason, to recall this resolution. The word of God will stand when they have talked against it never so long: we may destroy ourselves by dashing against it, but we cannot destroy or frustrate it."[8]

The question then is this: Must every man that will be saved by Christ be willing to loose his life for Him? Do only martyrs belong to Christ? I answer, we may safely affirm that none are saved but martyrs: either those who are actually martyrs in the flesh, or those who are martyrs in heart. To be willing to offer up our lives for Christ is part of that saving change which God makes in the heart of a man at regeneration. This is what bearing the cross for Christ, following Christ, is all about: "Having faith enough to encourage and love to constrain them to be martyrs if the honour of their profession should require it."[9] David Clarkson wrote: "To be fully, heartily resolved to bear it, is a kind of bearing it before it comes. And in this sense there may be martyrs who never suffered death for Christ. If they be so resolved to die for Christ as nothing hinders but want* of opportunity, they are martyrs in heart, though not in act; the Lord accepts the will for the deed in such cases. When the mind is so resolved on it as nothing hinders the deed but want* of a call or occasion, the Lord looks on it as if it were done. A disciple

* lack

thus resolved to bear the cross, will be accepted as one that bears it, though it be not actually laid on him. But he that is not come up to this full and sincere resolution to part with all, to suffer all for Christ, he is not so much as a Christian intentionally; he is not, he does not intend to be, a disciple of Christ, whatever he may pretend to."[10]

Thus the doctrine that has been developed is this: *An attitude of martyrdom is fundamental to all genuine Christian profession.* Those who profess to be followers of Christ, but love any one thing more than Christ, deceive themselves if they suppose they will be recipients of eternal life. Instead they will be among those Christ speaks of in Matthew 7:21 who will cry to Him, "Lord, Lord" at judgment day, but will be cast into hell for all eternity.

The first application of this doctrine then applies to all who name the name of Christ. Do you love Jesus Christ more than all else, even your own life? Search your hearts openly. John Gerstner has said, "Every one of you there has to be ready to die for Christ, whether He requires it or not. If you are not a martyr, at least potentially, you can't be a Christian."[11] What in all the world is most valuable to you? Your family? Your money? Your reputation? Your own life? Only by comparing your devotion to Christ individually to other things that are precious to you will you be able to arrive at a genuine answer regarding your condition before God. If a thief in an alley pointed a gun at your heart and demanded that you give up your faith, would you be willing to deny Christ to escape? If so, your faith is not real. The human heart is deceitful above all else. Make certain that yours is not deceitful relative to your eternal destiny.

The second application of this doctrine is this: Self-denial in this life prepares us for whatsoever will come upon us today or tomorrow. No man is sure what the future holds. We may, in our lifetime, see a time of persecution unlike the Christian religion has seen in centuries. Are you prepared for such a time? An attitude of self-denial in all our ways will aid us in preparation for suffering, should it come.

A self-denying heart esteems the base things of the world little and loosens a man's affections from delighting too much in anything here below. Thomas Hooker wrote, "So much as you prize a thing, so much you are grieved for the loss of it; a woman that marvelously esteems her child, when she loses her child, she loses her life...so he that esteems his honour (as the ambitious), his life (as the natural man), his honour and his life are his gods. Take away his god and he sinks. But a self-denying heart places no worth in these; if riches be gone, there is but a shadow gone; if life be gone, there is but a bubble broken."[12] A self-denying heart counts all things as dung that it may win Christ (Philippians 3:8), so the one who possesses such a heart is not troubled if he loses all for Christ, for who is upset with the loss of dung?

Each step taken in the way of self-denial here, prepares us for the next step. In contrast to this, every time a lust is indulged makes it that much easier to sin the next time, and who knows but what our next sin may lead us to hell? Is not self-denial in every area of life implicit in Paul's command, "Whether, then, you eat or drink or whatever you do, do all to the glory of God" (I Corinthians 10:31). Matthew Henry in his *Commentary on the Whole Bible* says, "We must *accustom* ourselves to all instances of *self-denial* and *patience*. This is the best preparative for martyrdom. We must live a life of self-denial, mortification, and contempt of the world; we must not indulge our ease and appetite, for then it will be hard to bear toil, and weariness, and want, for Christ."[13]

Thirdly, if an attitude of martyrdom is fundamental to all genuine Christian profession, then woe be to those who will not even give up their lusts for Christ. Is a man likely to spill his blood for Christ when he will not give up a base lust for Him? Is a man that is more concerned about his reputation than the cause of Christ likely to die for Him? You that will not give up your love of money, selfishness, lustful heart, profane speech, or drunkenness for Christ, what hope have you of heaven? If those in Matthew 7:22 plead on judgment day that they prophesied, cast out demons, and performed miracles in the name of Jesus and, yet, they are rejected by Christ, then what will you plead?: "Lord, we were greedy in Thy name and lustful and drunk in Thy name." If you think you may live as you please as a "carnal Christian" and be admitted to heaven, you are greatly deceived! Hell will be your eternal dwelling place, unless you repent.

I close with the words of William Pink: "But what reason had I then at this time to trouble men's heads with such a thorny discourse of martyrdom? I answer, the habit of martyrdom, as I have showed, is included in the most fundamental principle of Christianity, love of Christ better than ourselves, self-resignation or denial, and therefore they deserve no answer but silence, who shall think a discourse of it at any time to be harsh and unseasonable."[14]

---

[1] A. W. Pink, *Studies in the Scriptures,* July 1932, p. 160.

[2] Richard Baxter, *Baxter's Practical Works, Volume 3,* (Ligonier, Pennsylvania: Soli Deo Gloria, 1990), p. 381.

[3] David Clarkson, *The Works of David Clarkson, Volume 1,* (Edinburgh: Banner of Truth, 1988), p. 451.

[4] J. C. Ryle, *Holiness*, (Welwyn, Hertfordshire, England: Evangelical Press, 1979), pp. 167-168.

[5] Anthony Burgess, *Spiritual Refining*, (Ames, Iowa: International Outreach, Inc., 1990), pp. 136-137. Reprint of the 1652 edition.

[6] Ibid, p. 140.

[7] William Pink, *The Trial of a Christian's Sincere Love Unto Christ*, (Oxford: L. Lichfield, 1657) p. 201-202.

[8] Richard Baxter, *Baxter's Practical Works, Volume 3*, (Ligonier, Pennsylvania: Soli Deo Gloria, 1990), p. 431.

[9] William Pink, *The Trial of a Christian's Sincere Love Unto Christ*, (Oxford: L. Lichfield, 1657) p. 211.

[10] David Clarkson, *The Works of David Clarkson, Volume 1*, (Edinburgh: Banner of Truth, 1988), p. 452.

[11] John Gerstner, *The Parable of the Ten Virgins*, (Orlando, Florida: Ligonier Ministries, 1988), audio cassette tape message #3.

[12] Thomas Hooker, *The Christian's Two Chief Lessons*, (London: T. B., 1640), pp. 87-88.

[13] Matthew Henry, *Commentary on the Whole Bible, Volume 5*, (McLean, Virginia: MacDonald Publishing Company, nd), p. 669.

[14] William Pink, *The Trial of a Christian's Sincere Love Unto Christ*, (Oxford: L. Lichfield, 1657), pp. 226-227.

The author is indebted to William Pink, whose sermon on Luke 14:26, first published in 1631, provided both the inspiration and some of the descriptive phrases used in *The Gospel & Martyrdom*.